# My Tranquil War and Other Poems

**Also by Anis Shivani**

*Anatolia and Other Stories* (2009)

*Against the Workshop: Provocations, Polemics, Controversies* (2011)

*The Fifth Lash and Other Stories* (2012)

# Praise for
*My Tranquil War and Other Poems*

"When I first plunged into Anis Shivani's *My Tranquil War*, I had the impression two of my most admired dead poet friends were one-upping each other in the afterlife—Tom Disch with his straight-faced drop-dead virtuoso satire of literary and political pretension and Aga Shahid Ali with his eloquent, global, polyglot formal legerdemain—both of them knowing more about history and about literature than ninety-nine percent of their readers. But Shivani's poems are no phantoms, they are vibrant, new, knowledgeable, daring, and welcome."
— **Marilyn Hacker**

"*My Tranquil War and Other Poems* charts precisely how literature begets politics and empire becomes pariah via colony. Surrounded by canonical figures old and new, poet-provocateur Anis Shivani has written a book where best and worst are marked by their complicity. He has described the world where we all—uneasily, ultimately—live. This is a book of fierce intelligence. Read it and weep." — **Claudia Keelan**

"Formally inventive, confrontational, and erudite, Anis Shivani's *My Tranquil War* calls upon us to rethink our view of a war-torn world in which the ages-encompassing conversation of Literature and Culture is both bulwark and catalyst. Shivani writes about our hypocrisies and braveries with ventriloquistic precision, his gestures sweeping in history, tradition, and geography. 'I have to pay my accounts,' he writes at one point. 'I thrive on excess. // There is that lampless house. / The path unlit, and the pirate's / sign swaying in the wind.' This is a provocative and skillful collection, one I will return to with pleasure." — **Kevin Prufer**

"Anis Shivani evidently inhabits a world in which every moment of time in the past, present, and a humorously but lethally prophesied future, occurs simultaneously and is animated by a wit sometimes subtle, sometimes savagely indignant. Its two faces join forces and somehow manage to speak in unison of what they actually see and think (thereby breaking the first law of correct adult behavior: never say what you actually think, not if you like eating and having a place to live). I sense everywhere an undercurrent of compassion and identification, a poignant humanity and sense of responsibility underneath the torrential voice of his book." — **Franz Wright**

"Anis Shivani's *My Tranquil War and Other Poems* is a complex, ambitious, and formally inventive collection. These apersonal poems, often political, always erudite, are sharply interrogative of the literary or political figures and events they address. The war here is one of consciousness, of mind, as the poet takes on the compendium of Western culture. There's a unique sense of the poetic vocation at work in these poems. I can't think of anyone else who could have written 'Elegy for the Bill of Rights,' a powerful sonnet that evokes Jefferson, Nietzsche, the academic world of *Areopagitica*, to end vividly with 'That mummy melted in winter is us.'" — **Rebecca Seiferle**

"This is daring poetry, critical, a history of art and war in the modern age, it's 'man read[ing] man to swallow him whole.' Anis Shivani tempts you to call him by a name you think you already know, as his poetry shifts you from Robinson Crusoe to Robert Creeley, Dean Young to Virginia Woolf, Stalin to Fellini. There is a multitude of voices here, a history of a voice perhaps, documentary and fiction, writing his own language which is also ours." — **Fady Joudah**

"There is multiculturalism and there is interculturalism, and the unexpected sights they promote are stanchions of this book. Shivani studs his work with unexpected views of older eidolons: Whitman, Pound, Cheever. A book of surprises." — **Michael McClure**

"In his poems of reportage, Anis Shivani watches the horrors of history play out ghoulishly like sporting events. But mainly his writing seeks sanctuary by looking poetry and its makers (and a stray president to boot) squarely in the face. Pound, Whitman, Virginia Woolf, even George Bush. Though his Whitman is big and wide I ultimately think of Anis Shivani as a detail man, a miniaturist even, at heart. In his 'To Robert Creeley' he nails it best when a creaking sign at night does awesome tribute to the man." — **Eileen Myles**

"Anis Shivani careens among the idols and obelisks of twentieth-century culture like a maniacal bumper-car driver intent on smashing art and politics both into submission. There is hardly a stanza in *My Tranquil War and Other Poems* that does not take aim at an iconic filmmaker, painter, politician, novelist, or fellow poet, and hardly a poem that misses its mark. If 'knowledge is a builder's harmony,' then Shivani has constructed a monumental edifice in verse—part Taj Mahal, part World Trade Center—to memorialize our times." — **Campbell McGrath**

"I admire the poems in *My Tranquil War*. These are wonderfully intelligent, allusive, interesting poems in an astonishing variety of forms. Shivani ranges freely through history and cultures, always alert to the salient moment, the sharp insight, the provocative point of departure. Here is poetry deeply involved in the writing that has gone before it, even the painting (as in the beautiful poem on Thomas Eakins). The poet moves in and out of other texts. His own voice, however, remains firm, distinct, wise, ironic, meditative. These are poems to read and savor." — **Jay Parini**

"If Robinson Jeffers had cable television and twenty-four-hour news, this might be the sort of poetry he'd write. Anis Shivani writes from the stance of poet as correspondent, attuned to history, politics, philosophy, literary chronicles, and aesthetics. *My Tranquil War* is alert to both the inspiriting and darker consequences of culture on every continent and in a vast range of traditions. I admire this book's deep concern with how warfare, brutality, and mass crime corrode the imagination and strangle humanity. *My Tranquil War* makes the case, again and again, that it is the responsibility of poetry to confront state madness and human violence with intelligence and acuity." — **David Biespiel**

# My Tranquil War and Other Poems

Anis Shivani

The New York Quarterly Foundation, Inc.
New York, New York

NYQ Books™ is an imprint of The New York Quarterly Foundation, Inc.

The New York Quarterly Foundation, Inc.
P. O. Box 2015
Old Chelsea Station
New York, NY 10113

www.nyqbooks.org

Copyright ©2012 by Anis Shivani

All rights reserved. No part of this book may be used or reproduced in any manner whatsoever without written permission of the author. This book is a work of fiction. Any references to historical events, real people or real locales are used fictitiously. Other names, characters, places, and incidents are products of the author's imagination, and any resemblance to actual events or locales or persons, living or dead, is entirely coincidental.

First Edition

Set in Adobe Garamond Pro

Layout and Design by Seth Cosimini

Cover Art: George Grosz, *The Grey Man Dances*, 1949, oil on canvas
29 7/8 x 21 7/8 inches, 76 x 55.6 cm
GG2680 (David Nolan Inventory Number)
Used Courtesy of The Estate of George Grosz, Princeton, New Jersey

Author photo courtesy of Mehnaaz Momen

Library of Congress Control Number: 2012932116

ISBN: 978-1-935520-58-0

*For Mehnaaz*

*My Kobita*

# Contents

ACKNOWLEDGMENTS / *xiii*

**APATHY**

Harold Bloom's Old Age / 19
The Death of Li Po / 20
To Michelangelo Antonioni / 21
Satyajit Ray's *Aparajito* (1956) / 22
John Ashbery's Discovered Childhood / 23
The Natural Modesty of the American Fiction Writer / 24
H. G. Wells Initiates Fiction Writing, Circa 1895 / 25
Perpetually Ascending GNP / 28
America Conquers India / 29
When Dean Young Was Young / 30
Voltaire in New York / 32
Small-Time Fishing in the Bay of Bengal, 1970 / 33
Zulus in New York / 34
The Women in My Household / 35
What the Holocaust Means Today / 36

**AROUSAL**

Stakhanov / 39
The Birth of Stalin / 40
The Revolt of Islam / 41
Wife-Burning in a Modern Calcutta Suburb / 42
Propaganda / 43
Billy Collins Confronts a Herd of Mexicans Caught in a Trap / 44
To John Cheever / 46
Memsahibs in India / 47
An Address to Walt Whitman after Reading the 1855 Edition of *Leaves of Grass* / 48
Salman Rushdie Detained (and Deported?) by Homeland Security / 53
Andrei Konchalovsky's *Siberiade* (1979) / 54
The Enigma of Arrival / 55
Robinson Crusoe / 56
To Robert Creeley / 57

**MADNESS**

Ezra Pound at St. Elizabeths Hospital  /  61
Nabokov's *Lolita*  /  63
Letter to Jack London  /  64
Godard's *Pierrot le Fou* (1965)  /  66
Spectator at Gandhi's Assassination  /  67
India Conquers America  /  68
Reflections of Gavrilo Princip at Bohemia's Theresienstadt Prison, April 1918  /  69
I Watched Executions Last Night with My Sister  /  70
Why We Make War  /  71
Fellini's *8 1/2* (1963)  /  74
Observations of an American Woman upon Donning the Chador in Tehran  /  75
The Life of Virginia Woolf  /  76
Modernism on File: Writers and the FBI  /  77
Warriors in Drag  /  78


**WAR**

Orwell Shooting the Elephant  /  81
Thomas Eakins's *The Swimming Hole* (1885)  /  82
At the Simla Hill Station, June 1910  /  83
Remembering Manzanar  /  84
1941  /  87
The Unquiet Vietnamese: Phuong Past Pyle and Fowler  /  89
Reaganesque  /  90
The War in Iraq Poses Irreducible Problems in Identification  /  92
Dear President Bush  /  93
My Tranquil War  /  95
Twenty-Six Angles of Surmise  /  96
Ghazal: War  /  100
The Abu Ghraib Images  /  101

## ENTROPY

To Derek Walcott / 105
Lottery / 107
The Fifth Year of Our Fabrication / 108
Response to Pound's *Kulchur* / 109
Elegy for the Bill of Rights / 110
Juvenal's First Satire / 111
After the End of Books / 113
To Djuna Barnes, on *Nightwood* / 114
Normandy A Posteriori / 115
Conversations with Autism / 116
New Orleans a Year After Katrina / 117
At the Intersection / 118
Upon Viewing the Enchanted Mesa at Acoma Pueblo / 119
Jean Cocteau's *The Blood of a Poet* (1930) / 120
To Edward Upward / 120
The Essential Salvador Dalí / 123

# ACKNOWLEDGMENTS

I would like to thank the editors of the following journals in which many of the poems in this book were first published:

*Agenda* (U.K.): "Nabokov's *Lolita*" and "To Michelangelo Antonioni"

*American Literary Review*: "To John Cheever"

*Barrow Street*: "Normandy A Posteriori"

*Boston Review:* "Lottery"

*Blue Mesa Review*: "Billy Collins Confronts a Herd of Mexicans Caught in a Trap" and "Observations of an American Woman Upon Donning the Chador in Tehran"

*CrossConnect*: "When Dean Young was Young"

*Confrontation*: "Memsahibs in India"

*Creosote*: "Upon Viewing the Enchanted Mesa at Acoma"

*Denver Quarterly*: "Twenty-Six Angles of Surmise"

*Fence*: "Modernism on File" and "To Robert Creeley"

*The Fiddlehead*: "At the Simla Hill Station, June 1910"

*First Intensity*: "Why We Make War"

*Fulcrum: An Annual Journal of Poetry and Aesthetics*: "Voltaire in New York"

*Harpur Palate*: "The Women in My Household"

*Harvard Review*: "After the End of Books," "Elegy for the Bill of Rights," and "Letter to Jack London"

*Interim*: "Remembering Manzanar"

*The Iowa Review*: "I Watched Executions Last Night with My Sister"

*Los Angeles Review*: "New Orleans a Year After Katrina"

*Margie: The American Journal of Poetry*: "An Address to Walt Whitman after Reading the 1855 Edition of *Leaves of Grass*," "Intersection," and "Wife-Burning in a Modern Calcutta Suburb"

*Mascara Literary Review*: "The Death of Li Po"

*Meanjin*: "Propaganda" and "Small-Time Fishing in the Bay of Bengal, 1970"

*North American Review*: "Stakhanov"

*North Dakota Quarterly*: "The Natural Modesty of the American Fiction Writer" and "Orwell Shooting the Elephant"

*Notre Dame Review*: "Dear President Bush," "H. G. Wells Initiates Fiction Writing, Circa 1895," "To Edward Upward," "The Unquiet Vietnamese: Phuong Past Pyle and Fowler," and "Warriors in Drag"

*Pacific Review*: "Conversations with Autism"

*Pavement Saw*: "The Fifth Year of our Fabrication"

*Poetry Northwest*: "The Abu Ghraib Images"

*Prism International*: "Salman Rushdie Detained (and Deported?) by Homeland Security"

*Rosebud*: "Zulus in New York"

*Runes: A Review of Poetry*: "Spectator at Gandhi's Assassination"

*Salamander*: "Robinson Crusoe"

*Stand Magazine*: "Reflections of Gavrilo Princip at Bohemia's Theresienstadt Prison, April 1918" and "Response to Pound's *Kulchur*"

*Subtropics*: "The War in Iraq Poses Irreducible Problems in Identification"

*The Threepenny Review*: "John Ashbery's Discovered Childhood," "Satyajit Ray's *Aparajito*," and "To Djuna Barnes, on *Nightwood*"

*The Times Literary Supplement*: "The Revolt of Islam"

*Verse*: "My Tranquil War"

*Wasafiri*: "America Conquers India" and "What the Holocaust Means Today"

*Washington Square*: "To Derek Walcott"

*Xavier Review*: "The Enigma of Arrival"

*The Yalobusha Review*: "India Conquers America"

*Yemassee*: "Harold Bloom's Old Age"

"The Essential Salvador Dalí," "Ezra Pound at St. Elizabeths Hospital," "Fellini's 8 1/2," "The Life of Virginia Woolf," "Memsahibs in India," and "Modernism on File: Writers and the FBI" are found poems, heavily borrowing and adapting from the original books.

I owe tremendous gratitude to David Biespiel, Marilyn Hacker, Fady Joudah, Claudia Keelan, Michael McClure, Campbell McGrath, Eileen Myles, Jay Parini, Kevin Prufer, Rebecca Seiferle, and Franz Wright for their generous support of this book.

I am also grateful to friends and teachers who offered words of encouragement early in my career, particularly Forrest Hamer, Tony Hoagland, Brigit Pegeen Kelly, Li-Young Lee, Adrian Matejka, Natasha Trethewey, and Elizabeth Willis.

Many thanks to all the editors who have published my poetry over the years, particularly Rob Arnold, Judith Beveridge, Wayne Chapman, Danielle Dutton, David Hamilton, Brian Henry, Major Jackson, Wendy Lesser, Robert Lewis, John Matthias, Robert Nazarene, Benjamin Paloff, Martin Tucker, and Sidney Wade.

Of course, my greatest gratitude goes to my publisher Raymond Hammond, for taking a chance on this book, and for backing up his iconoclastic vision for poetry with real action.

A special thanks to Ali Eteraz for always being there, and to Gary Heidt for being a good friend over the years. Mehnaaz insisted on our first date long ago that I take my poetry seriously; without her this book would not exist.

# APATHY

# Harold Bloom's Old Age

In my hands, the canon found a friend dear,
I pray; my memory-stained evening candle
fanned the fire Cervantes lit, and Shakespeare,
and Dante and Keats, all who'd manhandle
trivial fate in its fiendish sparks of life.
It was not a consumptive Mann I met
on that Magic Mountain, or in the strife
of Venice, where death was the strangest fête.
No, it was a summer shower, when Wilde
whispered in praise of my fleshy memory:
You'll have prophesied our God-wounds, dear child,
you'll have lost our collective victory.
Oh, count me your strong acolyte, your fan!
I've shadowed the lively symbol's wingspan.
If I've lived at all, I've counted my breaths,
as each day I've murdered my sad Macbeths.

# The Death of Li Po

Li Yang-ping, preserve my poems. The emperors,
on whose behalf I wandered, are jealous like wives.

To travel a thousand rivers upstream or down, in a
moon's half cycle, is only to deliver one's true debts.

In Ch'ang-an, the winehouses gave me a special name
I both abhorred and loved at the same time:

Banished Immortal, meaning he who imagines life
as a continuation of the mountain's other side.

Long ago, in the gibbons' shrieks I heard in K'uei-chou,
a passage of sorts was enacted. I lost my strangeness.

Now, on this river that beckons to the civilization
still remnant in the shrunken land, land of half-sight,

I embrace the moon, its diffuse wavy pattern, its
silken bodice, its talkative-silent recital—a poem

inherited among the thousands I most love,
to live through the tough interrogation ahead.

Li Yang-ping, preserve my poems. If I drown,
in the brown depths the poet's only disguise flutters.

# To Michelangelo Antonioni

The window dwindles toward a seeping horizon,
tainted and black—if only color were to emerge

as a friend between me and the holy partners
who have cautioned all scripture to existence:

a man plastered to a white wall as background
draws the lines of Verdun in a fevered grin

which reminds him of priests going insane,
without causing distraction in saving routines.

Once window-shopping used to bring relief.
At midday the sun was a cause for swallows.

We inaugurated peace studies with hallucinogens.
The blind among us inquired of the longest journeys.

How a man and a woman lie to the bedroom walls,
as though inarticulacy were a matter of pride,

and how we exchange identities with inferior
subordinates, as though war were freedom's only

reward, speaks well enough to our descending
into a street grid with few exits marked as such.

# Satyajit Ray's *Aparajito* (1956)

In an India grown old by the hour, boys
have a hankering after travel to the new

parts of the world, where men and books
cohabit a future of unprophesied signs.

Where a sacred river goes to die in sludge,
and priests are taught from the cradle on

to turn each misfortune into truth's fire,
it doesn't take much to freeze ardor.

A boy grows into a man and retrieves faith
for the camera's squared scrutiny,

and finds only the bed eaten by worms.
It is a liberation, if only into finitude.

A mother's love settles into the field of dust.
In a rainless summer, the insects crumble

like paper atoms, dry as the sated earth.
And the wide world sells love to orphans.

# John Ashbery's Discovered Childhood

The police were here, and they were searching for a cop car.
They've seen, in silent breakfast trays, evidence of a crime,
sunless and discreet, whose trail leads back to a hungry Christ.
Fine, I tell them, scrape the mountainside brush for penny-
clues; fine, go ahead with your stethoscopic nose to grimace
verbal flexion into your trademark tone deafness. The police
tore down the wayward weather-favored tufts of filament-struck
clouds. They also hit my bamboozling grandmother of the crosswords
with high-water political dogma: whatever passes for law
is the law, etc. Afterwards, I had hot tea in the dark library.
My mind jumped from book to book of the Berlin thirties,
when disgust with self was always at hand, viz. Grosz
and Isherwood. Why do we not have such talented mockers
today? We only have placentas rocked with booze,
waitresses in thin religious headdresses when they're off work,
sportsmen beating up the thick cabin walls in Minnesota
woods to make them echo, echo, echo with the denouement
the common man has figured out. I have run pretty low,
and it shows on my ringless fingers, taut like tiger claws.

# The Natural Modesty of the American Fiction Writer

Never a debt acknowledged to *Appointment in Samarra*
or *Arrowsmith* or *Revolutionary Road*: not to his taste
the exactitude of ambition of a not-so-long-ago era,
when careers were made and broken in critics' haste.
Where there is on the map Pennsylvania, he sees a hole.
Negritude went the way of the failed blockbuster movie,
and this was before New Orleans declined the dole.
Mother and father were both doctors: how groovy!
Some aunt in his family read—or wrote—he admits.
In the course of the interview he talks of Europe
soon after the war, when America cashed its chits.
He dealt with Vietnam and Nixon with heavy hope.
It could be the Indians and Chinese are remaking the tongue.
If they are, it's not a familiar tune, not a song he's sung.

# H. G. Wells Initiates Fiction Writing, Circa 1895

**1.**

The boiler, penumbra to rheumatic washerwomen,
reclines in turgid steam, present to its own order,
and the adipose quotidian miracle of the master's house
remaining alive in this same order, day after day,
conjures a comatose fantasy of wellness.

**2.**

The Thames a burglar's whole check.
Passive boaters would not know how to take in a resplendent moon,
should it occur out of time.
Hearts beat like thick sludge.
Who takes measure? Who keeps time?

**3.**

At the smaller lending libraries in Putney
volumes of girls' romances are dog-eared in what must surely be
acts constituting the antithesis of romance.
Reading has to acquire its passionate following of would-be grotesques and silent rogues,
or else wither of overuse, of course.

**4.**

Thomas Henry Huxley, Darwin's bulldog, retools young scholars
in his own laborious image, scholars to a new age
of dog-eat-dog, and youth at any cost—
oh, I am Faust, I am Faust!—who love to tell the tale,
and I one of those scholars at South Kensington,
before T. H. got ill, and I too in his image,
became a buried flower, before my time—
no churchyard stone to sing of how I came to be.

**5.**

It can't be literature.
I am no Verne. I am no James. I am no Conrad, even.
The *Pall Mall Gazette* is a gasbag of the golden age.
Man reads man to swallow him whole.
A new question about Victorian England:
Who will bury the cosmic corpse,
at whose expense?
Serial rights set the bar to profligacy,
though I thrill in this new proficiency.

**6.**

England, behind the city's scenes, smokehouse and workhouse,
bread and butter on the cheap, machine work never easier,
the hedges trimmed by knives sharpened through instinct,
mothers embosoming workhorse sons by night,
bewitched swallows sorting industrial rust,
new plagues infesting factory floors,
alleys dark hours after noon—
and myself no social observer.

**7.**

No, Mr. Ford, in the kingdom of letters
only boilerplate counts, only how you boil the common man's
astute sensibility.

**8.**

The discovery of the future is a prophet's melodrama.
It serves the earth-based ants right.
On the edge of Bloomsbury there are witnesses
to Carlyle being a sort of Quaker who preceded his time
by many millennia. Such strong will
in the face of menace and worry.
God's creatures are nothing if not aged.

**9.**

It is a time of fantasy and fable.
The century has proven elastic beyond measure.
Do we not behold democracy's final barricades
falling before our eyes? It is a time of fantasy, indeed.
Then there will be a future to reckon with.
Iron wills and iron skills,
for an age of prophets thrilling with palsy,
and weapons that dignify death
by its sheer quantity.

**10.**

The grotesque is a paradigm of beauty.
See how the failed chemist from the Potteries coughs blood
but keeps it secret from the housekeeper?
We travel through time to meet ourselves
in an earlier state of disguise.
And it is wondrous how often our disguises are intact after piercing.
Wondrous is the state of brotherhood,
as England travels through time, salvaging workmen's finest crooning hours.

# Perpetually Ascending GNP

Unburdening Tennessee mountain-skies faint, then repaint
our polyester faces (denied since the seventies, Wal-Mart homes
vacant for boomeranging jibes), our nylon faces stripped
of gesture. Wall clocks empty the sound of sound, troubled
of the noise next-door as mice in flotillas sing hosannas
to the daily bread—which arrives in uncountable fat loaves
in the hidden morning delivery truck from a Lolita heaven.
The five circles of gratitude revolve around my chubby face,
ravaged by gravity, lined as a used-up Dylan song. Then frowsy
neighbors with hair done up in rollers argue with the soaps:
Why won't the clocks sound strikingly (sane and ponderous)
as in our grandparents' days? Those were the days! Panoramas
of flirtation during company picnics refusing to unfold by script,
executives in red foulard ties and blue suspenders inserting
their jabbing fingers in their loose waistbands: I'm not yet drunk.
It takes a lot to get drunk when the nation is at war. Graduates,
sit and take refuge in the emperor-president's speech, disrobe
yourself of benign platitudes (those you learned in Shakespeare
and Plato), we're about to launch into the journey of (corporate)
life where you find your umbilical cord stretched to infinity.
It's a poetic world, ready-made verses scattered on the pavements
like so much victory confetti. Always the fat mice sing hymns.
Have you, on a broad starlit night, when the moon is a serenaded
lady with a smile wide as the oceans, paused to ask under the old oak,
Who should be credited with making "relativity" not an in-joke
among tweedy profs, but descended to the level of the sitcoms and soaps?
Have you thought of taking out a life insurance policy on the commons?
The icebergs? The galaxies? The thin ruminant strand between
haunted mouse and haunted mouse? The gravy on top of the paycheck?
I was a battered wife (metaphorically) suffering from a short-term
inferiority complex. The churches then resumed the reign of Victoria.
It's a sure Crystal Palace we've built in the immunity of glamour.

# America Conquers India

Swallows the Ganges     Of ragheaded cows embarks on numerical
          Statistical econometrical probability estimates: they will live
Or die. One or the other.     Conducts mortality surveys in public
          Hospitals. Is told the doctors are on strike. Hunts them down
One by one, until          Swallows the Ganges, all over again
          This time to keep it down. In Bombay prostitutes bleed
Of a new one, not AIDS, not any known STD, and the surgeon general
          Goes in with a C-130 full of bandages that fall out the back
Door. The back door is not needed in India. It is a corrupt country
          With leaders of short sight and Swiss accounts. America
In the interim, while the perfect anti-nuke government is found
          In the countryside—far away from Agra, for the Taj
Is now known to have infecting marble, infecting the poor with rumors
          Of royal wealth, therefore it must be banned before we do
Anything, anything reportable and actionable          For future
          Generations of Indians     Water will be purified
Toothpaste available in large cartons     Convent schools will be
          Publicized. America is good at publicity.    Madison Avenue
Will categorize          Oh damn, swallow the Ganges again

# When Dean Young Was Young

A fiery man dousing clothes of spring water and rose
looks deep down criminals' tubby tracheae. Gullible
terminals—my label for lugers of cancer on the Riviera—
spring in bed each time the windows lash amorally
against the storm-God holding them secure. Fetish
of foot and ankle, feather-bound phrases in French
and German, goulash of whiplashed sun-worshipers,
accumulate like truncated reindeer with teensy horns,
lost on the prairie before natives take over to dance.
Have we come so far that centuries of recent vintage
are blocked out of suburban view, and high-school
history teachers have to resort to biographical aids?
Have we in fact lost the currency of reason, whereby
ghosts could circulate among us as people? Visions
that used to befall my stricken grandmother, when
she was still able to pull wool over my sister's eyes,
are encapsulated in the Campbell's soup can, not
the Andy Warhol version of it, but the real thing,
piling on itself in the shelves at Safeway. Inside
the soup can and its siblings are politicians' swathed
noses. Outside the store, on a windy day, paupers—
my word for welfare dropouts and Vietnam fantasists—
corral into their rusty pans scraps of paper delivered
by newsmakers' divisions of leftover news. Whistling
at the growing, gigantic sign proclaiming the mart,
a pair of housewives in rollers tries to escape unloved
in their Karmann Ghia, but the sign becomes watery
red, and reads their mind. There will be a hungry cop
to stop them well before they speed up to thirty-five
in a twenty. There will be nosy inbreds and Edna's
calisthenics in their living rooms to prompt acrimonious
debate about the merits of eating crawfish or shrimp.
This is only one house, whose interior I'm familiar with,
as a matter of neighborly courtesy. There may be others
beyond the ken of chemistry and biology, Kantian
propositions coming alive at the last electoral moment,
hustling among the hustlers like labia within labia.
Who among us has not torn up Aunt Miranda's notes

to self when she was throwing up in Daddy's bathroom?
Who hasn't known what it's like to bail out cousin Jimmy
on false charges of possession of pot, in violation of all
that Jefferson thought? Gunrunners deny upon capture
by the feds that their world headquarters are Amarillo,
Texas. Tax-cheaters in Chicago, operating for Capone's
grain-handling successors, date only pensive blondes.
The vacancy signs have been up in the Midwest since
Mondale refused suicide pills. When I was a boy in India—
my moniker for unread Mann novels and Crusades histories—
monkeys dressed up in little girls' clothes exposed
their privates as if it were the latest European fashion.
Still, the motels around Delhi—my euphemism for me—
were filled with tourists escaping Floridian winter.
Space is a question mark with no intervening signs.
Time is erosion of land-grants awarded in absentia.
One starless Swedish night, hugging the Nobel,
I might shoehorn into my speech, for McMurtry's sake,
what made Cybill Shepherd in her prime the girl
we used as waterslide, inside the confines of Main Street.
Not even Disney alludes now to fascism's seeds.
I've wondered if there's a fountain, not yet belly up,
that generates automatic writing for the eternally
blocked, its water rust free, sweet.

# Voltaire in New York

A painter's dream, to live on in infamy,
has surprised our hero. He persists
in channeling Locke and Newton through mists
of journalese, and fails each time, but laughs
it off, chalks it up to experience.
He has fans, oh yes, women of voluptuous
proportions, who smother him and mother him,
and feed him buttery toast, and ask him news
of his aristocratic ancestors. *Mesdames*, he sneers,
*I never had a lordly bone in my body.*
Those kings then, the ones he used to dine with,
what rocks do they suffer under?
Are they dead after all?
It seems that on the subway panhandlers
detect him as a veteran alien,
and leave him alone for that reason.
The kindness of thieves surprises him still.
On a new day, a golden morning,
he takes in the Statue of Liberty,
refurbished, burnished, guaranteed.
*Ah*, he sighs, *I see the cycle ending now.*
It was a long way home,
but it is good to feel the opaque water
lapping at his stockinged feet.

# Small-Time Fishing in the Bay of Bengal, 1970

Five nights now we have traveled the mouth
of this estuary on the Jamuna, as I perspire
dragging the nets, trawling the wave south
of rupchanda and hilsa, herds that never tire.

My mates on the dinginauka sing old Tagore,
his odes to the breath and gloom of stalwarts
building the nation, while I question this lore
for only sampling how the watery grave hurts.

Our ancestors came this way and were content,
we are told, stitching frayed nets and fixing
the leaks in the boats, their future already lent
to the moon that preys on love, any odd mixing.

Tomorrow at sunup I will taste the oils in the Bay.
They say men and fish unite in love of the first ray.

# Zulus in New York

Mother, help me out,
the bangles are shutting off
the blood flow
to my wrists.
My ankles hurt too
from so much ambling.
The sky I haven't seen
in days of sightseeing.
Who is this man,
with tall hat and long boots,
who follows our every move,
as if we were thieves
out to pocket
a bit of their country?
The streets, I now believe,
are paved with the shit
of cows that must have walked here
before our ancestors' time.
I can see my face reflected
upside-down in the dying
street lamps along the corridor
where those without a home
let the crowd haunt them.

# The Women in My Household

They showed me how to tie silken scarves over my head.
They cried on Friday nights, after the ill muezzin's beat.
I heard them through shuttered windows, as I threw stones
in the garden. The heat, the buzzing flies, the moldering

moon, it hurt to plan existence beyond the duration
of the next lesson. Language was passage to euphemism.
I used to say, for instance, when asking for a kiss or hug:
What more did the prince discover about Cinderella

when he had done with the meal? A cramp, an ache,
a sudden gripe in the bones, they thought of as punishment
deserved, from almighty Allah whose business it was
to be on the watch. I only begged to be one of them.

# What the Holocaust Means Today

Even the hardiest donkeys, stripped of their pride,
paraded in ancient times with head held high,
dreaming of carrots. Therefore we survive.
Could it be that Canada is the eternal nightmare
of the fratricidal brother, the one with precancerous
spots on his broad head, and loose suspenders?
I seem to recollect blood and gore in *Treasure Island*,
although the story was read to me by strangers.
It takes little these days to appoint oneself goddess
or charm mistress of the commonweal, bread or no
bread. All points in the Village converge on matrimony,
because the poets converse in the language of the demimonde,
in exchange for iron bars on their windows,
loaned by the state. Eternally, a cock crows
at the curled crack of dawn, and knows
the value of kowtowing to superiors
who rhyme ingeniously while mocking college.
Run, if you'd rather take the subway, run
until the lap of your feet echoes on the crowded platform
like the sound of doomsday made small
enough to comprehend.

# AROUSAL

# Stakhanov

I stand, nude as a statue, this coal mine
celebrated for what it does not tell
about men of iron, men queued in the line
to seize Stalin's favor; I will not sell
my steel-clad muscles, my brow of beaten
gold, my mind free of inquisitor's goods,
to the first bid. My labor will sweeten
whatever stands between the state's changed moods,
ill and gloomy most of the time, and I
alone in a statue, its inner shell,
a being expelled from time. How proud and high
our heads walking the mine gangplank, farewell
written in our eyes, the night already here,
dead exhaustion the only drug for fear.

# The Birth of Stalin

You could motor your way lost.
Through Gori's streets, river of amalgam swells,
phlegmic artifice contains distrust of old,
closer to Islam's minarets than Christianity's steeples,
yet birthing volleys of order.
Infertility's child, star of delirium, hater of sanctity,
are you the son of the explorer Przhevalsky
(whom you experiment with as icon in the sullen thirties)
or merely the secondhand seed of Beso Djugashvili,
who lived and died for a short time,
like the other posthumous breeders of this century's odd
heroes? Regardless, this fertile valley,
at the crossroads of West Asia and East Europe,
will never have a moment of regret
in the ancient turpitude we know as the future.
Only the stars mutter in their gallic arc.
Only the free-fed starlings gibber nonsense.
A Christian birth, a miraculous birth, a wishful birth,
on the whole, and many sage patrons
stifling vodka's dead rumors yearn to be
dealt, free of this full winter of fruits.

# The Revolt of Islam

Is in the nature of a circle that seems to drape around the Ka'aba,
    the House of God Abraham built in the fullness of reprise,

the black box of blank argument that stares down your defenses,
    until you come rotating back out of your anonymity;

and it is in the nature of stoning Shaitan, who sits majestic and frail
    atop the maidan at Mina, and absorbs your shy pebble strikes

like the prince of the hour he always is; and it is in the nature of slitting
    the throats of goats and cows and camels, on the day the hajj

ends, and men and women can return to clothes not made for the coffin,
    drop their rags of hedging equality and return to the trader's pride;

and it is in the nature of revolutions plotted on the cool marble floors
    of mosques at the poles of the earth, red and green and blue

extrusions of sensate pilings, minarets that shimmer in the hazy distance
    like cocoons that gave birth once, then trembled and stopped;

and it is in the nature of hoarse running across the flat plateaus of Arabia,
    in pursuit of the demons Moses and Christ left alone as too warlike

and realistic to make sense as text, demons that replicate in India
    and Algeria and wherever else Islam goes because of the hunt

that never ends and goes round and round in circles wrapping tracks
    around the Ka'aba and the Black Stone you must touch with your lips

and the empty spaces between pillars in the mosques that swallow up your
    prostrations if you so much as stall your concentration for a second;

it is in the nature of circling and running and never getting inside.

# Wife-Burning in a Modern Calcutta Suburb

Sixteen years, she builds a case against Plato.

Then, when the well-wishers came,
fleeing in embarrassment,
chapal lost, bindi gone, kajal scraped.

Gubernatorial decisions of faraway nurses,
in Shimla or Shalimar or Shangri-La,
as per Kipling.

A brute jungle-lust.

Organized religion, organizing circles,
with each one of which she tightens
the noose around her own neck,
ignoring the sparkling fire
with unintended effects.

# Propaganda

Where we are all women with a Chinese grocer's
rapscallion smile, and teeth of blood, and deal closers
in tight grasp of reality; where we resurrect
every nightmare noontime the vale of usufruct
that was lauded our birthright by the town's young bard;
where Aladdin sings with the lamp turned high to guard
our women and children in paradise's shapes;
where neighbor warns neighbor to kindly lower the drapes
before the self-knowing police come on a whim,
which of course always is planned to the wasteful brim
with runny clichés from the local horoscope
(equivalent to Trotsky being slaughtered with dope);
where night comes to day exhausted, moody, and vain,
to be greeted with Cheerios and sugarplums slain
in the cause of work, and morning assumes its self
as sexy bride, open at every pore, fresh off the shelf.

# Billy Collins Confronts a Herd of Mexicans Caught in a Trap

As I was putting on my khakis, right leg first,
standing at the edge of my unmade bed in clarified mystery,
trying to drown out the cacophony of announcers' voices
I'd dreamed of, in the television of my night,
trying to silence their auctioneer beats, their tear-soddened pleas,
I heard a commotion on the street,
voices crying, "Thief, thief," and fearful responses,
I think in a sped-up Spanish.

I like to work by an open window,
and sleep by it too.
I like to arrest the world in its act of entrance,
before it makes a case study of me.
I could have stepped to the open window, a few cold feet away,
and observed the stampede, like one of the guards,
godlike and benign, who oversee the daily delivery
of everything from tomatoes to pain medication.

The part of me that is not the poet-in-hiding,
that occasionally wants a foretaste of secondary unease,
made me skip and rush the stairs,
and in seconds I was not Billy Collins the recluse,
the man whose neighbors know him mostly as a spy
careful with words and careless with talk,
but Billy Collins the concerned citizen,
graphic depiction of reason.

I don't know what I'd expected to find.
Perhaps the capture of the gang at the end of my suburban Ohio street,
which has lately assumed a more terrifying guise,
turned from head to toe in mutants' maladies.
Perhaps the return of my next-door neighbor's cocker spaniel,
delivered from the place lost dogs survive in limbo,
intact and floundering, after five useful years.

Perhaps only a street conference gotten too loud,

between competing flower deliverers,
their bicycle wheels tangled.
Perhaps my editor, shown from afar, missing her tempo.

"Stand back!" citizen Collins was ordered.
The burly policeman I'd known for years—Hank—had his hand
on a megaphone big enough to shatter the peace
of civilization. "Stand back!" again.

My neighbors had looks of victory on their faces.
Whatever was to be seen was out of sight already,
in a police van, blue and spotless, the siren on its roof unblinking.
"It's all over," Reina, my Hungarian neighbor, muttered. "They're gone."
The van skidded off, its windows darkened,
and Hank waved at us, like the gruff Gestapo officer
one always sees in wartime movies.

Who, what, why, how—the when and where answered—remained
to be suppressed. They were gone, and I was not alone.
No one talked.

I would not have my answers.
When the sigh of relief rippled across the front lawns,
and the doors gently slammed back on a disturbed morning,
I sighed too.

Some mornings poetry flows as if from muse to muse,
without filter or charge,
strong as the mind of a bird of prey,
and the poet writes as if taking down notes
from his wise older brother.
On rare other mornings the circuit of wholeness
cuts out, and one senses winter in fallen leaves,
long before the official onset.
What kind of a morning was this?

# To John Cheever

In a time that couldn't name its violence,
you wrote of boneheaded swimmers and wives
plastered with guilt, negated our silence
of many wars, many styles, many lives
spent to build the great cities we think free.
The swimmer batters past ornate Tudors
in a vision deferred like the dead sea.
All radios everywhere leak thick rumors.
The commuter train hoards glib survivors
like camp denizens, takes them to Babel
where they get busy as advertisers
always seeking the transcendent label.
Who was on that train but your nulled ego?
You willed the suburbs' cancer to grow.

# Memsahibs in India

advantages of Indian servants where could you find charges with such devotion? of 1934, one lady was sitting in a daze reduced to rubble; Memsahib, what time do you wish to And the servants reciprocated in 1941, the bearer, the Mutiny, the Second World War, the Japanese were about to memsahib offered her shelter their *ayah* when Veronica One household duty which was even if the memsahib stayed in the weather which swept down on her tender typical establishment He watered a few bright flowers on the surface, but in reality (her father was an army officer) Many of the British helped provided dowries though the British moved so often withered them overnight and planted, and as long as the verandah, the lady of the relationship appeared feudal, trusted servants took charge of all the money Indian servants were in the great Bihar earthquake an English nanny wife of a member covered her head and wept servant who would produce breakfast traveling? on her lawn outside her house carrier appeared, salaamed, and asked, lowered himself to do the until his sahib returned; the gardener of one, the dockside if they came back, threw the money into the water, one woman remembered, birth of a son with the words, British women trying to produce, compound around a bungalow, called *doob* and hours of the *mali's* time, seeds, it was felt, pansies, larkspur, sweet peas, Indian flower bed, skillful gardener, English flower! as one lady exclaimed delicate plant under the hot Indian sun short stories about Indian

# An Address to Walt Whitman after Reading the 1855 Edition of *Leaves of Grass*

Brooklyn heart-minder, vagabond lusting after intemperate thirst, son
    of America, first and last among equals, secular in religion, secular in love,
gross materialist of the spears of grass and spirited leaves wherever the land is not
    rocky enough to kill vegetation, wherever figures of fun abide,
Chaplin of your day, Dewey before the wars, Twain's father and son, tear-shedder
    for Truman as he might have been before the presidency,
termagant to hypocrites with European airs, who later would enshrine Wall
    Street in the lethe-letters of gold multiplied by gold,
diffident preacher to women composing the land's organic music in difficult
    barns, and to men of the rough temperament listening to the quiet sunset,
teacher, priest, father, worthy matchmaker, doyen, dean, demiurge
    of democracy, key to the future, maker and unmaker of the universal implant
    called liberty,
chastened in your heart when presidents expropriated your pure
    vocabulary, and war left things worse than before,
and littérateurs in New York's rising towers shook hands with your still-living
    legacy and promised to deliver a word or two of pure Whitman,
believer in the rogue common aspiration of the man without education as he
    goes about educating himself in the tricks of the world,
only to unlearn the darkest of lessons, only to hoist his jaunty self on the fine
    pillars of the world's sole tabernacle the colleges aspire to build,
father and son to America's hopes, its patriotic wars and subversive hymns, its
    arrogance and humility, its democracy and tyranny, its esteem and want, its
    trouble and promise, its uncharted vistas of liberty landlocked on the
    marooned isolate continent, deep red like blood,
father of one and all, father of the man
    with womanly sympathies, and the woman with the man's tough heart
    emblazoned on her sleeves,

you, who must have been elevated, when you died, to the first ranks
    of the crowd-annoyers, there with Jesus and Rousseau, after your rough
    passage out of America,
you who had us sold your bill of goods, in that free country of yours,
    in that free century,
you who knew how far we had come and how far we still had to go,
you who predicted all our wars and our charities, our solemn oaths and betrayals,
you who chalked up on your board how tired we would be at the end of the race,
    and how free,

you who saw the vision of a world without difference, where to be one man was
 to be the whole world, owning its rocks and ants and serpents and mothers,
you who gripped the saleable whole future and welcomed it aboard with a shout
 and a yell and a whoop of reciprocal love,
you who toyed with America as the idea without template,
you who breathed well-chosen diction, coming from the plain man,
 into the overwarm cockles of the professional wits,
you who lived through our worst warlike moments of realized agony,
 and refused to disappear at the other end,
you who came once when our soul hadn't yet melded, when the chiseling
 was vigorous and true,
you, bard of the people, champion of the ordinary, sampler of ecstasy,

tell us, tell us now that a hundred and fifty years have passed, and America
 is perhaps an aged hag with a vast burden on her shoulders, when America
 is perhaps stooped and hunched and vertiginous, and might appear
 to beholders far and near like a personage who lived not wisely
 but only too well, flabby and flippant and ferocious,
tell us how it goes with you, tell us how America seems to you,
 if it's not the old hag with the gnarled face, angry and tortured,
 if it's not the grim old man with knowledge of the world encased in a closed
 book, staring vacantly at the far vistas disinterestedly, alone and unwell,
 unfed and grieved, livid at the crowd,
tell us how America seems to you, now, in this age of misery and cheer:

do we still contain multitudes, do we still admire contradictions,
do we still welcome the man of the unknown past from the flat prairie in our
 tallest constructions of epistolary definition, in the spires of Manhattan
 and the churches of Boston,
do we still elect as governors and senators, secretaries and presidents, men
 of the truant heart, who long to escape their duties at the first signal
 of the freethinking teacher,
or do we only elect taskmasters and joy-spoilers, elect of the God in their
 knowing smirk, convinced of the futility of idea and thought and diction,
 freed of the salubrious value you saw to the continent without end, forever
 discoverable in far corners as the very embodiment of the single man's lone
 ambition—

do we elect and imitate and follow and worship and encharge men and women
    who know America to be eternally discoverable, or those who think the task
    is done,
America charted as idea and spirit and feeling to its minutest gradations, so that
    only the husk, the shell, the corrosive body is left, and the heart ticks, ticks,
    ticks,
but it does so at the warrant of the head, the grossly exaggerated head, crammed
    with the theories of economists and psychotherapists, crammed
    with magazine feed and newspaper talk—
do we elect such as you would have hailed in the street as fellow Americans,
do we recite and memorize and sing such as you would have thought our inborn
    speech,
free of false dilemmas and dead constructions,
free of the ignominious Latinate and the charmless old country double-meaning,
free of cant and hypocrisy and telling unease—
do we hail as our speech and thought such as you would have expected of us,
    even this late in our prolonged childhood, which, mercifully, still lacks grace—

or have we disappointed you, rough man of the spirit, with our programs
    and agendas, our dissertations and theses, our arguments and books,
dedicated to the uplift of the weakest amongst us, the most alien, the most
    ignorant, those most insistent on their right to ignorance and alienness
    and weakness,
dedicated to the compulsion of their loyalty, in terms familiar to the undead,
dedicated to the inclusion of the worn-out migrant, who not long ago
    used to dream of owning the newest gadgets and gizmos, mortgageable
    durable goods to build consumer confidence, but now is a question mark
    to his distant employers, perhaps in some other country, perhaps on some
    other continent, perhaps in some other world that is not America,
    that is not its spirit of defiant inclusion—
dedicated to understanding where we failed the poor and the sick, the black
    and the yellow, the native and the migrant, where we failed them in schools
    and hospitals and the fields and the land, in the housing lot and the medal-
    giving ceremony and the anthem and the song—
dedicated to realizing an America that wanders in unannounced,
at the newest newcomer's Fourth of July barbecue or Super Bowl party,
in a whisper,

in a soft voice,
making few demands and delivering even fewer promises—

is this the America you expected to find, dead but not dead, alive but not alive,
a cauldron of rumors and uncertainties and ambiguities,
where for a man to be a nurse, in time of war or peace, is not the same as it was
 in your time,
because where the profits go we all understand without complaint, without
 shadow defiance,
without pro forma disgust, without recourse to poetry,
and where all the wars are being fought in our name, the world over,
so that America, America, America, the vision of your futurism, your heaven on
 earth,
is a land arguing its own quick culmination,
famished for attention,
high-spoken and murderous,
deliberative and wrathful,
godlike and pathetic,
dormant and windy—
America, America, America, a possibility that has closed off other known
 possibilities, so that the world's curious spectators see it as a completed project—

this, more than anything, this completion of the inherently uncompletable, how
 can you explain this, if you are a man of your word,
how can you explain the weariness and the slough, the lethargy that has
 overtaken the land, like sleeping sickness,
from the groves of California to the beaches of Florida, from the forests
 of New England to the deserts of New Mexico, from the Nebraska prairie
 to the Texas farm,
a uniform sullenness, a talkless speech, a declamation promising apocalypse—
how can you explain our weariness, man of the world, equalizer before your
 time,

how can you explain our plaintive high dudgeon when faced with the difficult
 and complex,
how can you explain equality running out of steam, so that faced with its
 realization in the world of work and education and family, it becomes
 its opposite,

a runaway beast, containing horrors the most imaginative psychotherapists never
 charted—
how can you explain equality converting us into the herd that imitates
 and follows the worst amongst us, the least American, the least
 Whitmanesque, if I may,
the least because they calculate our end and our fall and our being and our
 destiny,
when what they ought to do, to fulfill your vision, would be to step aside
 and let us breathe free and live out our godgiven right to idiosyncratically
 translate the universe's unknowable mysteries into one man's ferocious
 determination to make true what seems true
 to him—

how can you explain, bard, why we have moved so far from your vision by
 moving so close to it?

# Salman Rushdie Detained (and Deported?) by Homeland Security

Your bags of aleph-bey, like a Turkish Sultan's numerals:
Have you had it in you all along to ogle our Southern beauties?
Do you not know your respective place, in the horny bowels
of wherever it is we manufacture garments and towels?
Hunh! Gotcha! These gold-spined volumes autographed
by renegade mullahs—we're not using any oxymoron here—
were these bought with your own money? Is there not,
for Christ's sakes, a fatwa against transporting barrels of
homemade secretions, which you call the poet's muse, prose-
writer though you may be. *Acchoo*! Bless you! We mean
no harm, of course, holding your outsized head up for
inspection. We were told these eyes were new. We beheld
last night, after the last Delta flight, a red flare in the sky,
which may have been the devil's copious way of worship
in the twilight of the angry age. We relinquish violence
if it's in the name of idol-worshipers from fourteen or more
centuries past. Your carry-ons will be returned spotless,
sir, if you will do us the courtesy of fluffing your pockets.

# Andrei Konchalovsky's *Siberiade* (1979)

Boggy march through deft generations,
as tall evergreens are felled in pique,
hard work the walking relic's only gift,

old and young scoffing at white promise:
in dear times the lost dead breed legends.
On these truths is the new man built,

each generation the puppeteer's mark,
the heroic type animate with or without
Gorky. Only the frozen tundra breathes

something of the bureaucrat's ecstasy
at meeting the $n$th limit of the Plan,
only the devil's swamp smells sweet.

Men die as so many artisans of self-
love, incarnate in the forever broken
train of associations: peasants and nobles

alike unified in seeing past the rituals
of birth, grief, news, play, and death.
The future writes out of literature

the surplus man, burnt alive, buried.
O Siberia, your sons and daughters
have been reborn into history's maw!

# The Enigma of Arrival

First the Coptics came smiling to the Maryland shores,
drowning black cats, when they weren't worshiping
the bells that never rang around their knobby necks;
then came the Assyrians, settling around Boston hills,
digging in the land like raggedy rabbits run out of chase,
weaned of scraps, agonized by the shadow of their tails;
then came the Phoenicians, complete with identity clasps
strangling their thin throats, swishing their romantic robes
as if they were a nation entirely of loving kings and queens;
finally, the Huns, who chose Philadelphia to build
in the image of castles where murders are publicized
to maids not afraid enough of their raping masters,
so that harmony in the new world may prevail.

# Robinson Crusoe

Better emperor of Christ's lost untaught tongue,
Man Friday's banned commerce of sacrifice,
vanquisher of self-doubt in hangman's trice,
England's gospel of growth for the wooed young:
What island off the Caribs have we flung
aside while we discoursed of smart offspring?
What redemption in world's ships may we bring,
that you've not in your mind's crucifix hung?
I read you as child, and dreamed I was dead.
I read you as man, and ask if I live.
You loose anarchy in the subject's head,
when you enact empire in a cave's sieve.
Multitudes off an acre of grain fed,
if we our tamed fears forget and forgive.

# To Robert Creeley

Creeley, I'm an
immigrant. I cannot
measure such

exactitude without falling
off a cliff. I partner
with dead socialists

and robbed fascists
every evening when
my teeth

ache and my knee
collapses. Creeley, I
wasn't born in

some faddish manger
overseen by goatish
men in white

robes being muses
to my infant
screams. At times death

brings cartons of stolen
books in a cart
that runs over me in

my sleep. Creeley, I
have to pay my accounts,
I thrive on excess.

There is that lampless house.
The path unlit, and the pirate's
sign swaying in the wind.

# MADNESS

# Ezra Pound at St. Elizabeths Hospital

Translates the *Confucian Odes*,
source of misery to his captors,
doctors taking excursions into barbarism,
Bedlam and appalling uncooperative
nurses, dank, dark buildings remove
intestines as at a YMCA summer
camp, fearless reeking of the foul,
operation known as hoodlum's lobotomy,
injected with new product known
to produce shock, locked-up employees
write histories of mental illness,
as in her book *Hitler's Ovens*,
ill inmates receive fine poetry,
Ezra Pound is a federal prisoner,
a crazy traitor, a convicted traitor,
a mad poet, the school of public opinion
libels, uneasiness from Pisa,
high-paid attorneys shut out daylight,
translates the *Confucian Odes*,
in the middle of months of senility,
begin a vigil for bail,
begin a vigil for Mary Todd Lincoln,
name the wards after trees,
the "Chestnut" a spiral of iron stairs,
tiny buttons in kindly eyes and keys
to congressional visits, radio blaring
in the glaring of the silvery inmates,
sits Ezra Pound King George V of England,
back in his chair, head against a cushion,
*Dorothy! Drag up my profile in a semicircle*,
reckless art students transport Gray Ladies
to the sickroom, my Laforgue and
Greeks, my Tolstoy in the Chestnuts,
Oh God, Oh God, don't let them retire me!
*Pisan Cantos* by velvet ropes, Henry Ford,
sign in, epitome of the American hired man,
*Neither Eros nor Hesperus has suffered
wrong at my hands*, from the FBI building

at Tenth Street and Pennsylvania Avenue
take the Congress Heights bus to arrive
at St. Elizabeths, I seldom know vacations:
*books, arms, and of men of unusual genius,*
*the usual subjects of conversation between*
*intelligent men*, incarcerated in the long dim
corridor by the tact of administrators,
winter months in the gloomy hole,
When will this end? *Books, arms,*
*and of men of unusual genius,*
the perennial foe of the artist, the State,
electrodes are not quite powerful enough
to cause death, though the experimental room
is a fashionable dress shop, he won't contribute
to *St. Elizabeths Sunshine,*
Have you visited Ezra Pound before?
Yes.

# Nabokov's *Lolita*

**1.**

His nymph Annabel buried in Europe,
Humbert brings her tired remembrance here;
New England, playback to puritan hope
(strung between two dead worlds), screams murderous fear.
Charlotte Haze cow-straddles his scholar's mind,
the bridge to wherever lust goes to die.
In Ramsdale's streets education's great find,
Lo in loquacious silence, learns to lie.
But how does a man kill someone's childhood,
when guilt comes packaged in airtight bottles,
stuck to the mouths of lust-deadened teachers?
Freud avoids the road as the nymph does good,
choking dead knowledge off with her throttles.
She has seen Hollywood's censored features.

**2.**

Clare Quilty: whose doppelganger, whose ghost?
Humbert's chase, Appalachia to the West,
signifies his immersion in the host,
both gift and ruin, always close second-best.
The bleak motels are key to the road run,
because here is where Lo turns on her charms:
the only fit start to perpetual fun,
birthing games denied to sorry schoolmarms.
The climax, the escape, the murder, end
in childbirth's loop past the cold war's readers
(so quick to buy knowledge of carnal things),
the sole postscript to art's self-conscious trend.
Humbert spawns healthier bottom-feeders,
but nymphs will never ask for costly rings.

# Letter to Jack London

Eating raw duck, acting out Wolf Larsen,
on the *Snark* with Charmian to Hawai'i
and beyond, did you ask how your person,
sum of the Horatio Alger story,
would affect us earthbound followers-to-be,
who have to live on the great bursar's check,
and have never seen a yacht's golden deck?

Also, your sales in gargantuan numbers!
Hundreds of thousands! How do they relate
to the canon as critics' night plunders—
the hidden, the castoff, the steerage freight
after the masses seize most of the weight?
We are not used to such munificence
in sales, such best-selling magnificence.

Consider our narcissistic egos.
We were told writing is democratic
politics par excellence, and it shows
in our nude confessions, our usual trick
of mating the inchoate with the technique
of realism, for Average Joes like us.
But you fashioned your own myth of success!

Ah, the myth of the self-taught sailor-man,
oyster-pirate, Klondike expeditioner,
tramp on the road, the Kelly's Army fan
who both adored and loathed the petitioner
to capital! You as practitioner
of life as data for writing condemned
the text-based author as man's only friend.

We'd rather be prophets too, don't you see?
But we know our legitimacies, we've traced
the unknown serpentine family tree,
to our full satisfaction, and we've faced
the restraint of the laborer graced
with the abstract chance of mobility.
It is, in this age, our nobility.

Rabble-rousing boy-Socialist of the bay,
you're de trop these days. But your example
galls, even if in your own naive day
you were both great exception and sample
of art in capital's maw; we trample
on patrons at our families' peril,
and they have us well over the barrel.

You had quick worthy followers, Dreiser
and Hemingway, Anderson and Orwell,
and every mythmaker not a miser
with expression, who plunged into the well
of our subconscious, and found there a hell
of our own making. Now we want a myth
the uninspired common man can live with.

Your Valley of the Moon, agrarian dream,
was followed, I think, by the Ransom-Tate
cabal, and look what they made of the scheme!
Utopias end at forty; it was fate
you died then, intimate with your real mate—
woman, you wolf, sickened by the hearth's bliss!
We take none of your departures remiss.

# Godard's *Pierrot le Fou* (1965)

Once in a noir dream, I landscaped blob orange
riverfronts, yacht-free for gangster millionaires

(doubled in deceit), and found my timeless old
babysitter there, asking me if my children

knew I was dead already? I was a fly on the wall,
listening to the American filmmaker propounding

action, love, and violence as the end-all of style,
and in my caretaking of assorted inert corpses

I tried to corner my partnering doppelgangers.
It is a line of choler draining from Poe onward,

whereby the luster of Vietnam-like signifiers
reduces to mere understandable war crimes,

waterboarding and Uncle Ho's naughty niece,
my old Hitchcockian genre conventions now

far too complex for this late capitalist cinematic
mode. I bubbled to the surface crazy like one of

Balzac's obsessed painters, living on and on in time,
long after the boulevards were stuffed with workers

planning educated general strikes, perpetual war
against the capitalists, daring to compose positive

letters to the editor. Film persists in directing its way
out of form and material, resorts childlike to the stark

cool of the riviera summer, ignorant of pastel closure;
against the nuances of destruction, it guards the free.

# Spectator at Gandhi's Assassination

*Ahimsa*! A sound sibilant and atmospheric
meant for no jalsa, or God-fearing men
in the mood for prolonged discourse.

Violence shades into nonviolence
by gradations too pure to be defined.

Next day, a riot will burst loose.

How bad is a day's pea soup
for a man fed only on promises?

Then, memories of the salt drive,
homespun, sickness in prison
brought on by the little man
who refused to fill his shoes.

The final gunshot perfection,
home like the dead's prayer.

# India Conquers America

Dharma is everywhere  These words and others float
in the crumbling pipework in the White House and men
hatless and behind in their bills worship the only value
they've been taught to love  Patience  More patience
Some mistake it for karma   Is dharma action?
How about sanctions on bee-killers? Make the trail to
Utah, genocidal and unjustified, a wasteland again
so that no man may know what it is to come to
a dead end  Planet earth is a dead end  The itch
on the sadhu's forehead suggests impotence as he
sits doling out home remedies to desperate housewives
American men now love women taken down a notch
by profusion of anti-cosmetics  American women now
plant horseradishes in their little plots of land  Everyone
has a private garden  a meditation hour  time to play
and even if this means the decline of productivity to
before Great War times, even if this means that bill-
collectors and paymasters harmonize in rhapsodies
that have nothing to do with national unity, still
all the mermaids talking up Plath have been silenced
This land is ours again  Wisconsin dairy farmers thrive
When in Crete now a rural Italian dreams of America
he knows it is a stab wound freshly cleaned and swiped
Equal distribution of land is next  Plenty of food
for thought, time trickling down in measured jots
At the unemployment office the banter smells of doubt
as it should, the revolution of self having been finished

# Reflections of Gavrilo Princip at Bohemia's Theresienstadt Prison, April 1918

The tottering Habsburgs' Ferdinand, Archduke,
hater of South Slav peasants (I had heard),
died not by the motorcade's absurd fluke.
It was not Serbia's legends that murdered.

They were strangled by their arrogant act,
their detached prancing (humble as it seemed
then to some, grateful to be in their pact).
My bold pistol shot has Serbia redeemed.

I am not repentant. Why should I be?
Since when did individuals shape history?
Ferdinand was lost to a dynasty
six hundred years on in the spoiled mystery.

On that too slow Sarajevo morning,
when the thick crowd along the April Quay
was hypnotized by power (fools!), the turning
history took was meant to the very day.

The entente cordiale declares war by plan
prethought. As if accidents don't exist
in the high plane generals and emperors scan.
I still see poor kmets barely subsist.

Millions have since died in Europe's trenches.
But I don't plead. I am not the agent.
Assassination: a word that quenches
rebellion. When war ends, what has it meant?

Europe was the tinderbox I loathed so!
My parents taught me well not to fear fear.
As a boy, I came to this Sarajevo
to learn a trade—hammer blows I still hear.

# I Watched Executions Last Night with My Sister

The football field, where I used to cheer as a twelve-year-old,
had been prepared to accept the deaths of forty murderous men,

whose souls we witnessed exiting with the ease of needles
running out of thread. It was like kicking

in the style of Pelé and getting only the goal post
on your bloody shin, and falling twisted and embarrassed to the ground,

your playmates laughing over your sundered body, screaming:
he is just like his sister, Daud pees sitting down like his sister.

# Why We Make War

Countless swallows have fared this way.

A rumor, on a promenade, a man and a woman
in warm clothing, asking for the impossible,
happiness in a cold shell, a complete circle,
its pencil lines black and definite and sharp.

I once was a fast-talking poet in Nashua.
I learned the savage art of saving money on gas,
savoring the burning filter, tickling it to a
massaged death.

Wilson naked in his stove hat, Eliot burning his cathedral, Pound arguing with penny loafers,
a land only the past understands,
to reach which the future sputters out in incoherence
at the peak of its magnificence.

I knew a woman named Natasha from cold Siberia,
and she fed me impossibly long novels by exiles and freaks,
and they all ended in the word "No."

The shoppers wear invisible clown hats.
Many-sided whiskers.
Chins.

A Bulgarian princess I once knew was fond of globes,
basketball-sized, in that other dream world émigrés
postulate as possible; her daughter was a nun
dressed up as a teacher of Slavic languages.

Deliver us from sugar and fat, the populace yearns!
These expensive educations have left a bad taste.
The river is satiated with silt at its mouth,
refuses to be the prime site for the Sunday picnic.
Meanwhile, girls in training bras cry
wholesome tears.

Home's a cul-de-sac:
follow it past the bent oak, vacant temple of afternoon dogs,
past the choked creek littered with torn sneakers reminiscent of fatal border crossings,
past the vain hollow tomb where the mayor sits, and sits and sits,
past its position in the relativity of the universe,
past its timing as the sacred castle in easy reach of the commuter line,
and you will need no further directions.

My nose bleeds at night.
I shift postures on the softest feather pillow I could find.
Still the clock ticks too loud, still I want to faint.

Memory is a trick of nostalgia.
Ambition when we had it in bunches led us to a poetry stuck with pins.
There were book clubs, but no books worth reading.
The iconic iron gate at the Connecticut private school
you remember being darkened by lush ivy
was a dream fact, sutured in thread, smaller each day.

Darwin frothing at the mouth when the last bit of fossil
didn't fit, was no pretty sight, least of all to his mother, vain and wheelchaired.

Bring on the fight!
Let us dig our way deep into the trenches.
There is a way the circle of the sun becomes a plopping feather bed
but it takes genius of Pound's magnitude to discover it.

All the men have left through the same doorway.
The women, in hot white dresses, nurse martinis, waiting to be sick.
The children smash their tanks and dolls in the layaway corner.

For now, we can afford to leave the lights on.
Soon this town, postulated as actually existing,
on the border between Missouri and Kansas,
will see an eclipse pass over, and hardly anyone will notice.
We will presume chickens shedding porous tears,
assuming anthropomorphic status for a single day,
that lasts like the distant back and front pages of fat émigré novels.

Welders, swimmers, baton-wielders, summerers,
woe to the weak among you!

We are right in the path of the prime migratory cycles.
We look jaded. We look changed.
We presume prime ministers to be paupers.
War comes and reconciles us.

# Fellini's *8 1/2* (1963)

fantasy of Hades where, exclusively in the film (that of the traffic jam), and
so as to begin a new attendant, who has read Guido's sacred and profane love
upheld by Guido "mingle sacred and profane" and Christian, wife, mistress and
can link hands It is Rosella that "at bottom…" must include several in our system
William James in *Varieties of Religious Experience* identified with melancholy
Guido's fantasy of tribal farmhouse perverted and trivialized by first encounters
of darkness and light inspiration proves to be ambivalent glittering sea provides
worship, intimation is drained of the temperament of white smiling figures forming
a dancing circle resolving the conflicts, asks Guido, his marriage at the press conference,
the "suicide" as visionary artist Guido's spiritual creative process of spiritual death
Mass, processing as through *8 1/2*, Guido in its structure presents Guido to be paralleled
in ASANISIMASA Guido seems to find the authen- each of his alternatives to assert
itself our view of what has gone before the emergence of the vision his will to the
Church to escape from the wheel of the film his personal when Guido, in losing
the essentially religious nature of descent to which the vision Grace communion shall
not be born again (with conversion) variant of a visionary reality burlesque Hades
"ANIMA" or soul is staccato and fragmented consciousness is the most serious of the
childhood the image the underground the sequence of Guido the fatality of interior
oscillation to liberation to trace out this trans- accomplice then by the Cardinal *salvatur*
Allusions were exhausted to escape the dreamer on some planet in his flight Clearly
Communist Ideal Saraghina Guido is right "multiverse" the principle of inclusive—
an experience resides in the unfolding of life towards a view of its orbit by Guido's
attitude in the hotel seminary yet the dance of the prostitute of some primitive or
naturalist sensations talismanic significance a kind of graphological entire cast of the
film has its dramatic rightness remnant movement of which sickness becomes vision

# Observations of an American Woman upon Donning the Chador in Tehran

Black deliquescence, the melting of the heart-muscle
in its last inward twitch: forsaken by fellow women
too busy hatching the downfall of survivalist trees,
I've mellowed into a being famous for her agonies,
most of them unearned. Here's the damn payoff:
See how the walls splitting men from men are really
fakes, see how when the crow, ravenously starving,
wants to land on a choice bit of morsel, he does so
with a paltry shrunken conscience, and hops from
crooked foot to crooked foot, all sideways mockery!
See also the faint rumors of suicide that spark the curb
each time a man makes the split-second decision to step
away from the rushing cab, thus saving his own life,
this one time again, and all of tortured mankind's!
You detect chastened points of honor in fallback
chess moves, the boards of monopolized time-wasting
come crumbling down, and unseen other spectators
clap at every unheralded step of boys grown thin
on scurvy. You can make absurdity a cherished game.
You can eat whole horses alive, in this blindness.

# The Life of Virginia Woolf

A sinning half-brother who Duckworth-named, true to wounds,
damages the known facts of male brutality: irrelevant or nearly so;
the old ladies of Kensington not a word about the play utter,
the terminology of fondling dictational for you, Vanessa to

Virginia. Leaving for Greece in her pajamas opens a bizarre
chapter in landscape effervescence, builders yielding heterosexual
likenesses: Virginia might kiss Lytton or Roger or Clive or Walter,
but Leonard must discontinue his daily record-keeping of her

condition, which is guile about water closets and copulation.
Vanessa sees through her sister's air of contaminate nonchalance.
The first of the madness, restored by house-hunting, lyrical
Kew Gardens, aspects of the beauty of Cornwall, and unwritten

semi-transparent flower-bed novels. Airless blue vapor: effects
of sex, sex of Thoby, Vita's aristocratic boldness frighten
Virginia, who apostrophizes the city inexplicably summer-mute.
O casket of parody, literary history is never risk-free; daughter

of Leslie Stephen is divinely happy among beds of nasturtium.
I am who am not reticent who refrains out of laziness and pride.
For the remainder of their lives their friends would be dying off.
One of these days the suicide dream, Yeats's wondering look.

Am I a snob? In astute typescript, I expect Leonard to adhere.
Daughters of educated men, resent Cambridge, oppose it tooth
and nail, for Morgan Forster's essays are brilliant in childbirth.
Educate civilization being destroyed in Hitler's phallic rise,

as the tiring leaning tower makes her twitch for country survival,
the walk to the Ouse the happiest earth-green journey in years.

# Modernism on File: Writers and the FBI

The direct object of these readings was to unearth seditions
What of the figure and impact of the critic-spy or ghostreader?

Free from Ivy League intruders, and biographical-historical literary criticism
Articles on the New Negro summarized from Soviet newspapers

What Roth was doing to advance the revolution was rather meager
Hemingway's makeshift unit of bartenders, waiters, priests, pelota players

Which he proves by killing a Nazi spy and by fighting Lucas *mano a mano*
Who played the "girl" to his wife's "boy" in bed, who enjoyed sodomy

What had happened to the "pure lyric dreamer" in the futuristic forest?
That poets are nuts, and especially modern ones—in a small open cage

Twelve Million Black Voices given to expression under Sedition Statutes
Sluttish woman, Italian grocer, violent elderly, humanity gone wrong

Nothing has yet been said about the poem; Rokeysee, Rokeysee, Wounded Knee
Man to Brecht. I listened in to news from London over KHJ, about the Soviets

Potato-goulash, boysenberry tart, not to mention 1 case of beer, wine and soda
Klaus Mann made out a check on this account for $4, payable to informant

I have had to witness the gradual destruction of all I had built up in a decade
The memo begs the question, "Checked with whom?" Display books with impostors

Most Wanted: Claude McKay and the Black Specter of African American Poetry
The problem of objectivity: dedicates a whole monograph to analyzing the poem

Just because paranoids have real enemies does not mean they cannot also be paranoids
A poet enmeshed in a dilemma, hovers for a moment, pardonably perhaps

# Warriors in Drag

Sometimes they interrupt strangers in sleeping cars,
pressing their own chest wounds hard to make the last of the blood
ooze out, then signal to the corridor, and welcome in
the tapped-out beast: the horoscope reading then takes place
prior to delivering the message of hope, verse by verse a lyric flight;
sometimes in beginner's Spanish they lose track
of time, return to the Inquisition's first moment of self-questioning,
and find it wasn't adequate, it was too little, too late;
sometimes at the quaint provincial airport, in Burlington or Durham,
ignoring the black-suited, red-tied executives stepping
off their Cessnas with zip in their step and conquistadors' bloodful grins,
they want you to argue your stance on the most healthsome cuisine,
whether Mediterranean or Japanese,
and decide if glaucoma is genetic,
they want you to decide if any of the cards laid on the table are cards at all;
sometimes they show up as cats seeking immunity,
when you thought they were indifferent pets;
sometimes they are the fissile in-between space
cutting off nightmare from nightmare,
where a white netless vacuum breaks your fall to a two-bit thud;
sometimes they are the nurses with all-knowing smiles
rubbing their ears as doctors pronounce verdicts
based on questionable tests;
sometimes they clean up your home after you so that vacation over,
memories of Hawaii jinxing your work plans,
you stride on clean rugs pristine as the factory product;
sometimes they are the jokers on the Nielsen questions and the exit polls,
the intense outliers on analyses of spending on children,
the ones who buy stocks long after the collapse;
sometimes they help out foreigners in long lines at the post office,
making them address their letters to their own homes,
asking, Have you not noticed how warm it is getting lately?;
and sometimes they check in their own dead bodies at the poor people's morgue,
in the middle of the city where the railroad tracks become visible and loud,
and reassure the orderlies: We mean no harm,
but who can refuse the glamour of warm klieg lights, cold beer, polite television talk?

# WAR

# Orwell Shooting the Elephant

When he took aim it was with a quake
in his imperial stomach: such queasiness
works best with sub-inspectors, fake
little authoritarians—almost the distress
of a subaltern dominated by a pucca
sahib is evident in Eric's pale face,
waylaid by yellow eyes on the Mecca
whose road vanished too close to its place
of origin. But what he thinks of as the night
of empire is only its first dawn, its loop
over its own carcass to bid an end to fright
among lowly sub-inspectors who stoop
so low as to register the yellow eyes
noting their every action: as if natives
had the same emotions as Shakespeare's spies,
Wordsworth's swains, as if he who lives
by power raw and naked must pay a price
above and beyond the silt morning ache
when a millennium's work is dice
rolled on whim, icing on the cake.

# Thomas Eakins's *The Swimming Hole* (1885)

Woman is memory.
Her bloody torn rags have been sent home.
Clean, compatriots, clean your pieties.
It is a new Sunday.
Where is manifest destiny among strangers?
We meet to prolong fear.
There is a cycle of birth out there.
Amongst writers, it is a pattern.
They come before they are asked.
Will we meet again?
In similar circumstances?
Do not believe we won the last war.
There is vastness yet to comprehend.
Trade in the knowns.
Exercise vanity.
The male body at its stripped-down best.
It all boils down to it.
That, and a hint of dolor.
Postponement of continental grief.

# At the Simla Hill Station, June 1910

In the plains, the palanquin rides were always too short
(if bumpiness jars old memories to the surface, so be it).
James and Verna would remove their glasses in the glare,
shout poetic obscenities, yell peace to the King or Queen,
tote up the sum of our happiness and theirs,
and what remained was a pasture of emptiness,
reminding of purged mad cattle from end to end.
But here, in this slanted afternoon sun, at this altitude of
conquest, past surmises well-heard and obeyed,
there is no stolen spring in the widow's step when she orders
nobodies around. She knows her boys in boarding school,
in rustic Sussex, must sooner or later hear of indiscretions,
and if the letters be full of silences, so be it—so be it.
The Viceroy's niece reveals a studious gift of gab, which she uses
to plot sending down old colonels to their grief in the plains,
and the reporter for the *Times* is too changed to notice.
The munshis and darogahs pretend to no loyalty
they do not have. The chill wind bears a redeemable ill-will.
The parties go on so late at night the bachelors yawn,
with all of empire's terrible boredom, its magnificent sin:
These will be the days least written about, least recalled.

# Remembering Manzanar

At least the sagebrush, we know, smiles
at night, when the searchlights are on
(searching for the fight that was given up before the fact)
and the barracks pretend to be privately asleep.
Then also sunlight's stipples of arresting caution:
we walk to the laundry as if charting a path on some new planet's
roughened skeleton. Visitors say Tule Lake
compromises the essence of what our benign
superintendents have captured here: mental rock gardens,
spiritual shock lakes, unified temples and churches
where we sing of ourselves as child-Americans.

*Shikata ga nai.* It can't be helped.

A poetess among the white high-school teachers wrote
for the *Free Press* minatory haikus, warning of the
future landscape. The mess clean as a laundry's
backroom (my bountiful waterfront Seattle, from which
I was roused the deceptive Sunday morning of Pearl Harbor,
gangrenously imposts its foggy-clear outlines on vacancy),
the bathrooms swept fresh amid all the possible
individual overgorgings. The intellect seethes
at this grublike existence among neighbors
who become strangers at the first mention of
known secrets (was it your daughter the whore?
Was she the one who screwed the camp superintendent's
cousin, the blank-faced visitor from potato-fresh Idaho?).

*Shikata ga nai.* It can't be helped.

The intellect barricades against the grip the following
generation (lindyhopping and foxtrotting their little legs
to loyalty, to death in the 442nd, to scattering us out of
our West Coast ghettos) possesses on our Old World mindset:
it is a mere pastiche, an afterthought, as we take
the yellow threat (Banzai, Emperor!) amongst ourselves
seriously. We are a league of tired old men,
surprised by events. A Sunday morning transformed

by Pearl Harbor into something of a double enigma:
Why were there no immediate shouts?
Why did neighbor remain neighbor for the foreseeable
future? We sold our car to the junk man for a hundred dollars,
evacuee's right. Our heirlooms from Japan tied into bundles
and deposited in a warehouse we would never again see.
I think of the miracle of ordinary life (without the knock
on the door) as composed of small lies, which added up to a
colossal mistake, until we reached the dung-smelling horse stalls
at Tanforan, and there confronted our mean smallness,
among the absent traces of horses, put to bed.

*Shikata ga nai.* It can't be helped.

Let the inu squeal meaningless secrets to the America-jin
(this old Issei, bathed in the glow of rock-garden spirituality,
is actually a spy, an emperor-worshiper—Banzai, Emperor!—
is in league with a dangerous future, composes blunt haiku,
could one day challenge the rationale for our endless patience):
what does it matter? They too must plant radishes
and build camouflage nets for twelve dollars a month,
like me, the dog I'm supposed to be, the man in league
with a foolish past. My niece has relocated to high school
in Wisconsin, where they have seen few Japanese before.
*You were in school for three years in camp?*
*Welcome, welcome to the integrated world of science*
*brushing out the distinctions among men. Your eyes!*
*So solemn and buried. What have they seen?*

*Shikata ga nai.* It can't be helped.

Close confinement is Europe's madness, too mean for our
vast continent. It must all have been a mistake.
Then what explains why I still burn at night?
When they say "camp" now they almost seem to mean
summer camp, children losing innocence by the day
to harsh guards and early puberty. There has been redress,
and the old cataracted women have wept on the arms

of luminous pale-skinned presidents, weeping for
a past which disappeared like tiny maggots
cleaned by the loyal young.
I have a way of repeating.

*Shikata ga nai.* It can't be helped.

# 1941

War games come to Louisiana's swamp.
The combine harvester will save the year.
The army will step up before too long.
Europe's madness is still oceans away.
Pent-up wives dream of siren-red dresses,
and the summer runs to baseball's sure rhythm.

Joe D. gets his fifty-sixth in the rhythm
of a man saving his race from the swamp
newsmakers spawn. The Brown Bomber dresses
like no white man of equal size that year,
his cool aplomb never given away.
The sportsmen balm their fury hard and long.

The Japs may maul China, but it's so long
since our men died, we've lost the warrior's rhythm.
Is it for us to give Britain away
to the Nazis, are we to drain the swamp
of Europe's hates? Lindy is right this year.
War is a bitch that steals virgin's dresses.

Der Fuehrer, gutter-voiced and limp, dresses
as world's lord; what if the world is a long
holiday, as the carmakers this year
note, selling automatic shifts whose rhythm
is fluid like a fresh girl skimming the swamp?
Detroit has kept the war planners away.

One more fireside chat and I'm pulled away
from noting how my plumpish aunt dresses,
too young for her years, too close to the swamp
of syphilitic grasp, and for too long
love's mercenary, attuned to the rhythm
of destroying the dark days of each year.

They tell us this is a defining year.
We must put hard-earned innocence away.
The most plausible of all is war's rhythm.

Who cares how my foxtrotting aunt dresses?
We have been amateur fighters too long.
Gimbel's rubberstamps the continent's swamp.

This nude year the day of infamy dresses
up fate, carriers blown away in a long
new chapter, reinscribed to the swamp's rhythm.

# The Unquiet Vietnamese: Phuong Past Pyle and Fowler

**a.**

On rue Catinat, shoppers for tomatoes
at noon look skyward, and pause: no returning
French bombers whistling sky tunes, and God knows
the Americans have waited for this turning.
I have heard the Statue of Liberty
is of French design. If so, skyscrapers
near it must remain smelling of asperity
of a kind unknown to English drapers.
One thing becomes absorbed into another.
Of the four brothers in a room, always
count on the one who tears up, to smother
his conscience, to win. Expect delays
in fountain-square explosions, don't bother
finding little girls' arms in the litter's haze.

**b.**

Finding little girls' arms in the litter's haze
is what my sister does for kicks. I foretell
by the pool of coals in Fowler's first gaze
of the day if Pyle will now ring the bell.
I am made to relate the plots of movies
and plays in minute detail, as if memory
were a trapdoor in use, as if honeybees
buzz in high pitch only to melt emery.
But Pyle is a boy in search of a mother
who values the art of self-knowledge.
And Fowler thinks it too much of a bother
to pull the scribbling Grangers off the ledge.
It leaves me to charm my country as other
than what I sinned against as moral hedge.

# Reaganesque

**19.5 PRIME,**
**13.5 INFLATION,**
**21.0 MISERY INDEX.**
**Four years of this, better off dead**
**than red, I say to GE**

bring me your Michael J. Foxes captured in youth, red-tied and suspender-bound, repeating Hayek and Friedman, while up above the skies Star Wars, better known as…(silent, for they still hear)

"Ladies and gentlemen, I have just signed legislation

OUTLAWING THE SOVIET UNION
WE BEGIN BOMBING IN FIVE MINUTES

Almost shot
almost traded (arms for hostages)
almost inaugurated on a sunny landslide-beckoned day
when all Washington showed up in a buzz of boll weevils
and horrendously red Armani
almost a poignant remembrance
late in the century
of Peacekeepers and Tomahawks and zero options

**Niezależny Samorządny Związek Zawodowy "Solidarność"**
**Deutsche Wiedervereinigung**
**ПЕРЕСТРОЙКА**

*Contras, moral equivalents of the founding fathers, so are the Afghans, and whoever fights Iran, and maybe the dress-designers on* Dallas's *set, is it morning yet, is it a hot burning sun that hides the blemishes of seventy-year-old Bel Air matrons suffused with preternatural drink, and will you know when Sunset Boulevard has ended in downtown to become a barrio's first rumor, will you be able to separate Armageddon from its mere prelude, how will we fire the next batch of air traffic controllers, how will we rebuild the Pentagon to the tune of hundreds of billions in deficit spending, when voodoo economics will have become voodoo everything, how will we have new hides of Teflon, young and positive and all-American and simple yes-and-nos, sometimes all answers are simple, even if they aren't easy*

Uncle
Avuncular
Olympian
Unprepossessive
Gipper
Great Communicator
Uncle
Avuncular

He loved us. Like babies loved by doting fathers surprised at fatherhood in their sixties. He mattered most when we considered the Beach Boys, in their youngest and oldest incarnations.

Trickle-down. Trickle-down. Evil empire gone.

A desperate morning, when liberty's sign
was zeppelined on the sky, California's
elder statesmen figured the country's spine
had been rebuilt to new anhedonias

At the funeral at last. I fade into the sunset. Nancy, mother, Mom, Mommy, midwife, missionary, mine. Football hero from Peoria. Bane of welfare queens, rightly. Just say no. Tear down the wall. Make my day. Are you better off now? Is it morning in America? They say we have reached our limits. Just say no.

# The War in Iraq Poses Irreducible Problems in Identification

The strap on the shoulder could be a child.
Or a bomb. How can a pacifist tell?
The weather this month is serenely mild.

The AP correspondent had just filed
his last ever story before he fell.
The strap on the shoulder wasn't a child.

Martyrdom in Karbala is self-styled,
again, as vow to shed the wasteful shell.
The weather this month is serenely mild.

In plain sight of shopping women is piled
the maimed corpse of civilization's hell.
The strap on the shoulder must be a child.

Rations suffice; electric lights run wild.
The Tigris is pure white, Baghdad a belle.
The weather this month is serenely mild.

What need exit strategy when we smiled
as the whisper of doubt turned to a yell?
The strap on the shoulder will be a child.
The weather this month is serenely mild.

# Dear President Bush

We may have misread Oriental inscrutability together.
In your raucous school days, past the circle of the camera eye,
sullen spiders crept to the top of the jagged fence, and wavered in the wind,
a subject not worthy of a poem or a coffin—
so you chose only to watch, as did I.
Each day for you has been a day of rumors of changing weather,
but you square the spirit's chancy legerdemain
with a haughty horseman's stance all your own
(once upon a time mankind was fool enough to build gothic cathedrals).
I, as usual, watch and learn, my ignorance
magnified manifold as the ships come in,
carrying posters of dead sailors and their worthy admiral
fathers. *Will you be my friend, will we serve mankind
gratis?*, is the eternal question aspiring poets
must ask in the hours before dawn when a hesitant
interwar muse, choked with blue smoke and girdled spirit,
wasted from the first hour, dumb with degradation,
visits and revisits the traceable (simple arboreal) lines left on
blank unsigned paper. Will *you* be my friend, Mr. President?
I am alone, and have grown tired of reading
others' tea leaves, of declaring oneness with sad mankind,
always suffering from nacreous self-destructive contagion (hence pearly memoirs),
always blowing its hard-earned wealth on lazy self-portraits
it knows were not originals even when first found.
I have grown tired of revisiting museums and brothels.
We know you like to compare far-distant apples and oranges
by way of signifying a return to the discipline of the gymnasium,
if not outright hazing and bondage, we know you return
books on time, decry therapy, and pronounce salvation
on the burnt Western deserts, because to ponder
our insignificance on this torn-down planet is false modesty,
as all the best prophets have known in their bouts of doubt.
It is time to put the old books to bed.
What have they taught us but self-hatred and guilt?
When did we ever plant a happy seed in a young mother's womb
and expect it to return a payoff in similar coin—
surely not since the days of the plainspoken knights in hot burning armor,
refusing to see their reflection in the drying river's unclear

waters, the mean hours of their universal crusade
passing them by, so that soon they would all turn into
self-reflecting Montaignes (penpushers and pedophiles). Mr. President, you've defeated
hypochondria, megalomania, paranoia, gluttony, gossip, and death,
with one hard blow of your weightless persona
(weightless because containing the weight of the earth),
and made the work of future psychiatrists and historians
passable play—you've made a man out of wandering Camus
and his joyless mountain-lifting, you've made an admirer
out of me (until lately a no-good fellow-traveler swift to leap
onto the grooviest bandwagon), as I've learned to distrust
the bookish mechanics of hate. Sooner or later these witches' brews were bound
to overflow. What we've known is that you've lived
in our castle not as our king but as our slave,
expunging the blood from the libraries of wars,
and resurrecting compassion in a tangible, movable lump
as ready as the next fleshy morsel in mankind's
planned dominion. You have freed all *your* slaves.

# My Tranquil War

This latest Baghdad café, demented charnel,
home to homeschooled Tigris tigers
(otherwise plump fellahs in robbery skins),
charcoaled and burnt, oafish incense scent
nestled between *Buscando Amor* and America's
soccer team, is one where chess-prone
Nabokov, in a long-ago tiff with treacherous
Tzara, might have chosen to meditate
on the ruins-to-be, vaporish like Nazi dreams,
without the faintest trace of émigré posture:
only the slowly rotating white ceiling fan,
concave wings coated with thin ash
(of body parts cyclonically reaching ceilingward),
reminding of the day having gone on
too long.

# Twenty-Six Angles of Surmise

**a. Shock and Awe.** Bishops move fast on the board. Result, in fashionable parts of Indiana, where tremors from the lower Village are felt first, as hard as the place of origin: Kasparov loses, and gracefully retires. Who knew championship rules? The turf of NASCAR Dads who marry soccer Moms, so that Michael Jackson may be eternally locked up. Al Pacino tells Keanu Reeves in *The Devil's Advocate*, Don't let them see you coming. Confession: I've never played chess.

**b. Grotesquery.** False tones of blues, rap, everything that passes for hip-hop, including hip-hugging ripped-up jeans. The man from Hong Kong who claims to be the real deal, the dealer in antiques, hundred-year-old books whose stamina is deposited in unbankruptable Swiss banks. The wholesale godown burnt down at Christmas, and employees were laid off.

**c. Checks and Balances**. First kill the Chinese gunslinger. Mafia boss. Oriental scrutability. Oriana Fallaci on her hundredth unpublished interview, since she no longer publishes, is not heard from. The rape of children of the church in old Kosovo and Albania, trickling down a decade later to New York publishing houses. All the old bosses are dead of obsolescence.

**d. Accountability.** Simply said, machines taking over for the brain. A tiny Voltaire in fifteen electrovolts, antistatic battery not included. Please pass the warranty. It counts for a millennium, if the gods don't before that go to sleep.

**e. The End of History.** Goo-goo, ga-ga, the pink British baby goes, under the hot shade of the pram, circa 1929, while Virginia Woolf is still alive, in Bloomsbury, as an earlier phase of Orwell ponders getting himself in enough trouble to eventually write *Keep the Aspidistra Flying*, which for American audiences becomes *A Merry War*. And they say Jean Harlow anticipated World War II. And III. And IV.

**f. Gallimaufries.** A Vonnegut word. Before that, Twain tied up in knots, to get at the heart of the Hearst empire. Yellow journalism, such as a Connecticut Yankee might find in his own boned town, off Mystic River. I think Richard Wilbur writes formalist verse, but it's difficult to say, at times. Yeats used to leave no doubt. Then we burnt Dresden.

**g. Preemption.** How MIT students right before Christmas break plunge earthward from the roofs of residential towers, five stories high, and leak brain death on pissed-off concrete. Such a mess to clean up. Such a waste of investment. But I never met a rude Boston cop.

**h. Medievalism.** In *Titanic*, Kate Winslet is supposed to have turned into an angel, and Leonardo (no last name necessary) a shaman from heaven. Very fine jewelry, stored in a Bank of England vault. With no claimant. So what happens is depreciation of art. Things stored out of sight have irrevocable influence on things in circulation. I never watched *Titanic*.

**i. Observation Tower.** The stars are closer than we think. The stars are farther than we think. The stars are no distance. Please raise yourself six more inches on your heels. No, the mechanism is not adjustable. No, we don't account for smaller people. Astronomers are usually tall. Why? Because they eat extra amounts of carrots. Veggies in general.

**j. Relativity.** In the thirties, Harold Laski was a big deal. I think Lasswell too. Prose had not yet become impenetrable, except in physics and philosophy at the higher reaches. All the human sciences were comprehensible to the layman, that straw figure of the professorial elite, who when they have run out of things to attack turn on themselves, then as now, although not then with such vulgarity.

**k. Elections.** A dwarf in Afghanistan crawls out of some cave, and we bomb him back to death. Good, rest for another twelve months, and then incubation and rebirth all over again. A man with holes in place of his eyes still doesn't empathize with the woman who wears a burqa to walk downstairs to buy carrots from the haggard vegetable vendor.

**l. Prose Poem.** Arnold went home. Tennyson was dead. He read Byron with eyes closed.

**m. Genocide.** A Plaster of Paris figure in the shape of Himmler. His nose, his chin, his musculature. Then a quick trip to the Kennedy School, where an assemblage of peers, masters of the universe, bankers and lawyers, frugal nitpickers, dressed in vintage Brooks Brothers, argues on into the night about the meaning of conventions and norms, so that the end result is the suicide of Kasparov after all, and the relegation of Indiana to irrelevancy, except for motor sports.

**n. Fatigue.** James Joyce in the bathtub reading of the newest findings in madness studies. *Ha!* he twitters. They should meet Stein. Lusty woman, with heart of powder-fine bombast. *I think women are the better species. They anticipate the end of the world more often than we do.*

**o. Telepathy.** What Uri Geller felt in Munich after a terrorist attack he couldn't see coming. His métier turned out to be petty shopkeepers.

**p. Buddhism.** Angelina Jolie's breasts looking like they're full of milk, all the time, even when she's fighting off spirits in ancient Egyptian caves, with jujitsu moves and gyrating curves. Robert De Niro playing the buffoon for the right price. Michael Jackson doing the moonwalk from the guarded SUV to the guarded courthouse. Us watching.

**q. Baudrillard.** Inkling of rumors of refurbished cottages off some southern Mediterranean coast no one's heard of. And he's there first to take one.

**r. Investment Banking.** Charles and piggy Camilla taking a hike off the royal path. They find Piggy from *Lord of the Flies* smashed to smithereens at the foot of a bluff. They hadn't realized the coast was so close. It must be summer. In London, the news will get around. Those who need to know will already know. I don't mean to equate the "homebreaking bitch" with the most sympathetic character since Holden Caulfield, even at the level of paper.

**s. Poetry.** Oedipus Rex. Oedipus at Colonus. Oedipus Oedipus.

**t. Rational Expectations.** Jefferson was tired after doing all the thinking for the country for its next two hundred and twenty-five years. At some point, the lease runs out.

**u. Artificial Intelligence.** The instruments of torture don't basically change. Whatever Caligula did, we do at Abu Ghraib, and in Indiana's supermax twins. The eminences transfer knowledge amongst themselves from generation to generation. There are always the five hooded men, Democrat or Republican, to take over the baton in some secret society at an Ivy League college.

**v. Cloning.** In Europe today, Americanism is the disease. The cure is more Americanism. All sides agree on this.

**w. Humanism.** An embryo in an eminent cow preserved perhaps for its extravagant tits or tail. Machu Picchu ruins. All the scholars lament. The wails crack my concentration on Friday night at ten, when in the streets at Yale I witness ghosts conversing in code, and want desperately to catch on. But the earnest busy bees won't let me. I figure the best thing is to enroll in some science, or mathematics, or economics course, anything beyond my ken. Then I think of the "not enough women on the faculty" problem, and break down on the shoulders of my girlfriend. She says, Have you read Dean Young? Have you shared a glass of wine with him?

**x. Authorship.** Arnold went home. It's not on fire, never is. His library is bankrupt.

**y. Talent.** James Joyce in the bathtub, laughing at the calamitous news in the *Guardian*, because it doesn't lead off with Lawrence's affair with whatever married woman he happens to be fucking at the moment. Then the mad daughter herself shows up, and wants Daddy to show her how to cook a chicken.

**z. Totalitarianism.** Chomsky, meet Derrida. Arnold went home.

# Ghazal: War

We think of the thirties, expectant in the squiggly room of war,
as unrepeatable: never again that prearranged doom of war.

Hamadryads lounge in kilts—there, soldiers cleaning guns—
the obscene sceneliness inspires Parnassian boom of war.

Among kings and kingpins, logomachy is the timely art;
they say no sensuality overwhelms the wordy perfume of war.

In the narrow straits, the oil tankers have been quickly reflagged,
the reticulum of allegiances rewoven to the womb of war.

The secretary of state, in her hour of fame, brings the charts.
Her periphrasis disguises the revealed nom de plume of war.

O known and unknown soldiers, Samadhi, in sleep, is yours:
eternal sleep, where seraphs fly on the witch broom of war.

It is never too young to die for the homeland, never too gory.
At home, weaklings are enlivened by the purple plume of war.

You, Anis, logrolling joints, stare into the abyss of your Hallux.
In the closet sits your effervescent self, the bloodless costume of war.

# The Abu Ghraib Images

The zero seconds in the pulses
animating Goya's *Third of May*
have ceased: it is how we hood
the crimes of the past, how we
steal from classical conceptions
of pathos, irrefutably current.
*Guernica* doesn't do this justice.
Nor Milgram's prison experiments.
Something about the dark
solitaries crowding the ghost-rooms
of the imperium, something
about the thumbs-ups, the wide
grins, the signal-choked embraces
of the iced detainee, the textbook
postures (wires trailing from genitals),
is beyond instant recall, even if
familiar like the hair on our wrists:
we find this night slit open like
our favorite poet's suicide,
anomaly piling on anomaly,
making us afraid of shadows,
which linger inside these doors.
And the benign names—stress
position, sensory deprivation,
"fear up," "ego down," "futility"—
deprive us of rational bearings:
it is how we viewed the barbed
wires of our fortress cities
from the distance of fiction.
I hear in the pyramids of naked
men, piled in easy symmetry,
the accordion of religious zeal:
finally the equality of sexes,
the equalization of man and beast,
the erasure of borderlines,
we have been seeking
since Luther nailed his theses,
heralding the climax of eros.

# ENTROPY

# To Derek Walcott

**1.**

Start over Omeros, with a new sea.
The fishermen in St. Lucia have bargained
with the sunny devil to prosper among
friends. The very sand is choked with
lust. The islands send signals at night
to marooned in-between gods, who assemble,
drunk and smiling, to hear assorted
complaints. I have not known old and ugly
women, only their embryos when cool.
Blueness is a question of the seeing
entity willing to suspend disbelief.
It is impossible to grow up as an empiricist,
check values against values, expire
at night behind dark unfanned doors,
and argue with the trust of neighbors.
I give you, Seamus and Joseph, fellow sons
of history, *How to bend on locked knees*,
before the composers of civic behavior,
and come away ignorant as birth.

**2.**

Start over Omeros, with a new sea.
A roseate history lecture, pinned to the fins
of the roving sharks, whose blue vision
sparks the live islands' very marrow
and ends the drunken hangover
from the fifties and before, at last:
St. Lucia, of a Sunday afternoon, becalmed
like a lonely bride in her last moments of waiting,
will not yield her secrets to mere passersby:
of which more, intestate or not,
to follow, after the satirists have unfolded their
lawyerly pajamas and sagely sipped on poisonous
tea. Everything here channels tonnage
from afar, from Caliban's unknown travels,
from Prospero's fickle sayings,

from Crusoe's accumulated mistrusts,
so that in the end there is nothing left to see.
Yet the tourists come, bonded to cameras.
Yet the poets sing, in sugary tongues.
Yet the politicians breathe fire and ice.
Once, before ill-repute was for natives to own,
I sang of fishermen and their catch—
the evening stretching from horizon to horizon,
the very sand as though pocked with the holes of thought—
in a laughing voice, smooth and round,
like my neighbors' calculation of unfallen time,
all comparison of disuse allowed.

3.

Start over Omeros, with a new sea.
Your transcription of the dead Aegean
into the lush Caribbean cauldron, where the sea,
inundated by hopscotched peripatetic wanderers,
hollers in the single digits of the night,
*How not to worship Wagner's blond beasts,*
yet awakens a bad taste in the mouth,
knows the song of delight, sung in chiffons of salt,
murderous to the ears, yet clocked and heard
by all my sleeping neighbors. I have not known
such uncaring sleep, since those days of youth
when I first emerged into free-falling silence.
No, the walls of Jericho might not fall.
Apocalypse is for the continental bourgeois
who skip through the pages of history
as though through Gothic romances,
already knowing all the famous endings.
Here, a midsummer cloudburst drenches
our pig-sleep, creeping past pink death.
These offices have long remained vacant.
Child of illegitimate silence, I have willed
some nonpareil paradise to come into being,
and it only takes a man or two to put it
on the map where Europe never strayed.

# Lottery

*After Dean Young*

After Myrtle Beach, the new paradisial sins hung free
in the gambled-away air, corralled and beatified,
tosses to prone sailors. They were mad when young,
suggestive when older, and in the end foppish maids
growing into throbbing satin dresses. I thought
Simone Weil was a lazy murderess when not
nakedly swimming in the plasticity of ur-French
thought, dank and dark, like lovers spread on molasses.
Did you say Caesar's Palace was being torn down?
I hadn't heard, unless you mean its sensate marble,
which last time I looked had a pink aura of Eco's
fascism spreading over it, like a drunk Taj Mahal.
Has it shed its skin?—this would be the fifth
year in a row. Not that I care. I welcome all cats,
plump and thin, vomity or sedate, to my aggrieved
door, now that I have plenty of milk to give away,
in jars thick as barrels, as though I were building
wrestlers. None of my high-school sweethearts
has called so far, I expect because the phone lines
are thick with the same illness that infected my
father and his kind, who spoke always of hard work
as though it were Mormonism with guts. Notice
you hear Beethoven's spunk in elevators when you least
need him. A fake sky covers the motel room where
I awake unsuspicious, possibly in Alabama, or
could be Vermont in summer, as though shading
the terrestrial kindling to set the whole show on fire,
earth and its googled habitants, *Playboy*-hiding
men and their unbunnies, swimmers and their socks,
so that only a sawdust spread of melted humanity
survives. I was told clocks in this country are sensitive
to changes in wind and temperature. Will these
canceled checks suffice? Money is spent by owners
of Lamborghinis in past lives as though it were a dread
Foucault's last glimmerings of the author's existence.
Why then have I not yet made your acquaintance?
I am waiting, in a yellow pantsuit of a cousin's provenance,
if you are willing, if you are dying too of sudden
verisimilitude, which follows our coattails home, in gouts
of tennis-ball size, oozing and oozing agreeability.

## The Fifth Year of Our Fabrication

On the road braced with carping mules, it's been a long haul.
We've waited our deliverance at every turn.
We find corners, unturnable corners, and then blown leaves
of classics, newly humorous. Who knew Tolstoy was so funny?
I'm nearly every Chekhovian character with a penchant to cry.
I'm every male before mechanized bread-making,
with his head in the sand. And the sun won't come up.
It won't smile in the cozy cartoon manner of two-year-olds
denied articulacy. I find flattened replicas of the dour sun
every few feet when I keep my eyes on the road, as I always do
now. You've seen how old women have been fighting off slough.
It used to be they were caretakers. Overhead, in what they call
flyover country, planes sound a thunderous rumble, as if bringing
the sounds of the overpopulated jungle, to our shy corners.
High-school football cheers have the stuck-on lust of real war
taking place far away and in sunnier climes, where death is a postage
stamp left affixed to the eternal envelope. Our leaders speak
through megaphones thick as our sunblocked heads, their winsome
smiles copied from leisured shaves for workless days.
This street leads nowhere. We both know that.
And yet we keep turning to it over and over,
hoping there might be a sun-blessed ice-cream parlor at the corner,
a chirpy attendant there in love with his voice, helping us mix flavors,
whom we will tip handsomely, as the ochre paint of the walls
will stay in memory, only that, and the whipped Bauhaus chairs.

# Response to Pound's *Kulchur*

I am alert to your backward glance
        solving the promised land of our Adamses
but realize the truth in your fecund roast:
        Shakespeare does not repeat himself,
and the artist is the only one who can't fake.
        How will you handle, though, the new
Comstockeries, blooming from the lavish
        coastal soils like bully gospels
of culture? You speak of English decadence
        circa 1909, but history almost always
happens as an inflated guide. Plugging along
        in the mud of knowledge, buried in
faddish Rome, usurious as only constitutionalists
        aware of money can be, I fear the yoke
of universities dragged to dull liberty—
        not the Catullian irony you speak of,
not the remediable entry of science in art,
        not the gnostic nomenclature
of all of us as sons of Zeus, in Aesop's terms.
        It is a higher truth, parsimonious
civilization, you record, free from usury,
        yet here in earthly categories fixing
the factions, Hardy has been immortalized
        in the Ivory Tower, and man's benign
influence (as laughing animal) has exceeded
        any known study of physiognomy.
The weapons of the tiny minority have been
        seized, the curricula removed to desert,
*diorthotikon*, corrective justice, the bilingual
        gestalt's finalized craven terror.
I cannot find pimps enough in your closed cathedra
        against words westernized to technical
progress. And how will America yet pay its debt?
        Unwobble debt-free rallentandos, speed
Confucian pedagogy to the son's general home,
        pay the cost of commerce, mother of arts,
move mornings toward habit, name the theatres.

# Elegy for the Bill of Rights

No more, now, dear English professoriate,
does *Areopagitica* stamp the halls
as live, current news: the undergraduate
represses the last faint Nietzschean calls.
A dark unwanted night shades our green youth.
Jefferson strides on the broad frontier plains,
remodeling the beauty of the uncouth,
and we spurn this haunting as unearned gains.
A chill wind stakes the dignified household
where armies plot against good Senators,
clothed only in the redress of habeas.
Who among the prisoners will make so bold
as strike the sheriff who frees the haters?
That mummy melted in winter is us.

# Juvenal's First Satire

### *After Ted Berrigan*

The failing pussy-worshipers, to homosexuals by night,
read, read into the diluted cereal bowl of the wasted

Greenwich flux: who else but I will soldier for grants?
Peculiar and pecunious. Inebriated, we march, kamikazes,

pleasing Fifth Avenue's silk-laced window-voyeurs, to meet
more new inbred Whitmans. Must I suffer these crappy

juveniles singing of the multitudes every time I turn
my back against Mecca walls? All abstractness procures

limits. We don't know, in the midst of the Vietnam crime,
how many Nixons it takes to unplug the goth horror show

bled from Melville onward; but if Frost's reading that crisp
January morning at the Capitol is a sign, not much longer—

if the *New Yorker* lasts. See the VW's, their egg-
hides hurtling up the Adirondacks, mechanized in blue,

bicycles drooping off their roofs like used bra straps;
inside, booed family news spouted to muzak in mirrors:

Can you hear that sound? It is the sound of the rashest of
Pope's circle, ashen-faced before reason's nude congress,

evoking in sighs the drenching blood of the young century.
It is how we read today, in that knowing wink to Eliot's

hesitation, as though we were of the Promethean genus
barreling through department doors. But we are mute as

drugged cats, draping ourselves on aristocracy's banisters:
brown-fugged, prone to politics, reading like damn whores.

Ron and Ken and John, I need this Guggenheim reference
as a cow needs mulch, so will you shovel your last doubts up

my anus? See again how the Strand fills with lissome
(still a word?) blondes from Morningside, arguing over bad

Camus, as though it mattered which bed existentialism wakes
up in, as though the prophets will swoon and rest after '68.

# After the End of Books

An endurable childhood, now, without
*Bleak House*, without Jane Eyre's petulant pout,
chasing no Lilliputian dreams that stay,
defying no dangerous Fridays, only play
Estella in *Great Expectations* would
fail at—ah, I see, to define the good
gives me pause unless smuggled in from texts
hewn largely from shape-shifting bed-perplexed
inquiries of mystery (adult novel
jouissance-blessed as child's anti-hovel,
Kubla Khan's palace, Coleridge's dream).
Let the child transcend Werther's German scream,
meander through fair youth like no Hesse
navigator could. Let him pick the mess
of Freudian conflict on the shore of birth,
pulchritude and the sublime found on earth
quadrants close to his home. If we still get
Rastignac without the lessons to let
susceptible provincials learn, then Kant's
timeless dictum (men are ends, not means) grants
us peace. Apocalypse cannot be real.
Villettes will keep running to France to feel.
Wordsworth's *Prelude* returns, written or not.
Xanadu stages piles of rot upon rot.

# To Djuna Barnes, on *Nightwood*

At last I see your aesthetic quarry:
to trump the flood of lewd words O'Connor's
watery-grave mouth leaks, after horrors
we spawn as if the state were our glory.
I see how Nora's fealty is treason.
I see how Robin bowing to the dog
in the last hours of the blunt monologue
evokes the return of the dead season.
Djuna, are you vanquished, do you now laugh?
Women have chosen swords over deaf words,
dictators have unpaid armies for staff,
Guido the idiot self we kill in thirds.
They read you then as warbler of passion.
They thought you a fad, a passing fashion.

# Normandy A Posteriori

Ezra Pound wears three hats
each with a hole as big as the planet,
his way of noticing genetic drift.
Blue levitation on Vichy morning
when the milkmaid runs out
of the house screaming Life, life,
does it have to be so crude?
At dusk, Mercury is a dot
on the ground no brush
can efface. Capital punishment
is outlawed by three low judges
fed on porcupine's quills.
De Sade dances in the streets.
Billboards come down by night.
Paradise glances back, appeased.

# Conversations with Autism

Yesterday I balanced a sing-along bucket of pale reflective water on my head.
Long lines of strangers handed out food shortages amidst a Chinese sun, and cans
of ham, hard and cold to the touch, and the shove behind me evocative of Waugh.
I mean the strict sentences, whose every behavioral ecstasy is a surprise to the gentry.
I mean the naked Catholic insistence that foreign objects remain true to their pile.
When we burn the fire outside the church, none of the moth-eaten books are spared.
Why not melt words, when worlds have melted? The medications we take for sleep,
sex, and silence are prescribed by princes paid to objectify the gardener's toolbox.
My semantics are your preverbal ladders. My chance for victory came in 1914,
and I have not let up since. Here is a classroom, lit by 500-watt bulbs in November,
where surly scholars await a second Hiroshima, which they imagine will sanctify
their parents' daily fights. The television is staticy silent to caress, and the blank
screen a paid-for encyclopedia. Here is the crux: knowledge is a builder's harmony,
a music of pasture and pagan rites, a mound of sweet scrap I like to sit on just so,
like an actor out of work but sure of being first in line to play one of Lear's daughters.
Wouldn't you know it, I'm invisible the whole time? If I breathe, it's only as ritual.

# New Orleans a Year After Katrina

Perhaps there was a jocularity in the origin
myth we overlooked—perhaps there were talents
mined too deeply, hard-edged voices struck
too sharply against the violating timber
of sandless time: Now these ornate balconies
on Bourbon Street suggest a missing temptation
(how Rousseau in his *Confessions* outed himself
as a checkmated charlatan time after time comes to mind),
the walls having stepped forward a little closer
to the edge where known quantities have been
described, and the unstern black awnings looking more than ever
like afterthoughts not designed for fortitude.
The trolley on St. Charles is dead, the tracks
empty, the parade of noise among familiar strangers
shut up, as if the Gods were still seething (from the aftertaste of miasma).
The cemeteries have emerged from the flood
less possible than ever, the tombstones mere white stone slabs
with diluted engravings, and the dull pasty hand of muddy water
mocks chronology. The cemeteries have again been
buried. The penumbra of violent acquaintance
among the hastened citizens who remain
paints new sturdy Edens, even if pleasure,
for now and for the future we have written,
will never again come at basement prices.

## At the Intersection

The man who drives the Hummer
must be a bigamizing colossus from Egypt: the hard rap bangs
against the walls of the tactful ecosphere,
the bubble of shopping maniacs,
their ears closed off—the vibrating thunderstorm
too late by several centuries at its destination;
the man who drives the Hummer must have a foot-long
dick, so garrulous in its suburban researches, his wife
must be a worshipful blonde beast, eager to proclaim
her allegiance to Nietzsche's sister;
the man who drives the Hummer must have a job
feeding lions, regurgitating Livingston's prank in Africa,
the mirage of one lake meeting another,
and the tribesmen laughing at the happy impostor,
asking, *Have you met us, Chief, now, have you met us?*;
the man who drives the Hummer
must be in bed with the president's closest staff,
advising them how to maneuver the Middle East's
chess pieces so that at the end of the match
we might smile like conquering
Ajax, the field of slain sheep only a possible thought,
only a forestalled mistake;
the man who drives the Hummer
must know how it is to forgive his worst enemies
because he has won the only crusade that counts.

# Upon Viewing the Enchanted Mesa at Acoma Pueblo

This is not rock, silent rock, rock of time.
My footsteps echo the brute yellow butte.
Red afternoon wind, in the mesa's climb
to the sky, is a whistleless sigh, mute
like the tight embrace of the sentry stones.
What do they guard, these abutting bald rocks?
Ingenious man—hid from watchers, your bones
weeds round your hollow soul—distemper knocks.
This is the valley past the crawl of death.
Night has never lit here without regret.
Man wakens to the sun stunting raw breath.
You do not hear the footsteps trailing threat.
Once this valley absorbed all the red sun.
This energy is earth's core on the run.

# Jean Cocteau's *The Blood of a Poet* (1930)

The mirror, black as a dull headache in siren,
placidly sits along the gravity-defying trapeze

splitting this hour from the next, dividing hot
chess tournaments that end in gratuitous death

from mere spectacle, man and woman in love,
willing and able to feast on the corpses that result.

Invitation to the muse, who compels levitation
in defiance of motherhood, queerness to martyr

many childhood solaces, and the reversal of
death by gunfire, Mexican and statue alike,

is of cagey interest, blood spilled on the ground
named as such, thick and mottled, curdled on

the emitting skin, pulsing like fevered prose
dead off the pen. And always the vivid mouth

of someone else's buried dreams, offering
unwanted opinions relative to the artifice

of martyrdom and myth, the poet's need to live
along the thin continuum of lined-up keyholes

in the corridor where few depart to die,
opening up singular dreamworlds of pageantry

we thought died with childhood. It is all there,
contained as in packed metaphorless novels

one thinks populated Weimar Berlin's hovels,
an entertained voice of aggression, delighting

in the loge ceremonies our forebears perfected,
not caring to comment on the congealed blood

of the poet qua poet, his residential stability
sealed off from the many walking statues

constructed ex post facto in his honor,
when it no longer matters, when he is saved.

Hapless ballet ceremony of the naked side,
torn at the hinter-skin, ballet-engorged poet

sad in the nick of time, presuming to gesture
toward the hollow relatives and friends dead

in name and substance, is of retrospective
interest after all, the burdens of biography

aside. A cold draft wafts over disembodied
couch-creations, aslant and awry, surveiled

by spiraling hypnotic spheres, and partial
limbs reattach, assemble something of a poem

in how lead follows lead, or not, how bits
of thought are made to cohabit like torture.

## To Edward Upward

How slick the tuxedo-outfitters' dishonesty!
How astute the winners in investment banks' lunchrooms!
Old colonial memories, shared by colonels long out of distress,
evoke a vague collective miasma of nervous fritter,
which we are one and all glad to have stylized.
Everyone dresses now as integral widows at too-cold northern
seaside resorts, where gulls swoop down with loss of wings,
and magicians and clowns stop to admire painterly
stillness. Every man has been trained to think
mathematically. My fragile mother deserves better.
These days bones, teeth, hair, skin, membranes are first to go.
What is left is the filament-trace of the body that used to wander
nighttime hells, persist in advocating for the twilight idols
to take their place in the stately front of the audition room.
Chance, and its betters, have been victorious,
have pushed aside the programs of our youth,
and isn't it right that we are present at these denials of our friends?
Isn't it appropriate that not a one will admit to having fallen for
Stalin or his ilk? A purity without puritan hurt haunts
the new legends, as they dedicate their works to future generations,
asking only that they be read with a measure of forbearance,
and please to shell the pound or two for the glossy journal than circulate worn copies
checked out of public libraries. I admire their need-bruised wit.
There used to be women one presumed to be nurses.
Somewhere beneath white sheaths cold medicine lurked.
Could we have escaped the wavelike transitions from drunken decade to drunken decade?
The shops, as I said before, want to equip us in knightly armor
for our small domestic battles, and we mock Tolstoy's mockery
of Shakespeare, ascribe it to old age's crankiness.

# The Essential Salvador Dalí

### *Figure Standing at a Window* (1925)

The peaceful bay, at the window where she leans,
chastity in white, how we spend the summer,
before greater talents intrude, and we turn around.

### *Venus and a Sailor* (1925)

Already the diminutive male, the sailor in her lap.
Kiss the vague image, not the lips themselves,
kiss only the painted profile, not the substance of man.

### *Woman at the Window in Figueres* (c. 1926)

She is embellished by the fabrication of the town.
The balcony is a hothouse of gigantic suggestion.
Back turned to us, she contemplates the victory
of the mind never at rest, even in private lacemaking.
The town grows sturdier, the mountains sink down,
and the ability to concentrate is a jest to be coined.

### *Senicitas* (1927-28)

I perceive the beginnings of healthy paranoia
in your rendition of the limbless body, attacked
by spatters of red worm-fests, clouds of blood-anger,
shimmerings of a heady transvestitism beyond sex.
Lorca, of course, died of a shot to his headstrong heart.
All the bloodless submerged lactation in the world
won't give us our genitals back. The body floats
awkwardly, more male than female, in the synergy
of the corpse moments before it revokes license
to conjure possible monsters, donkeys of the head.

### *The Wounded Bird* (1928)

Breton dreamed of the bird that fell into the sea,
turning into a cow before dying. Your rough sand
extinguishes the fire of the heart, the bird a footprint
simplified like all death: the fall greater than the climb.

### *Unsatisfied Desires* (1928)

I wouldn't call it castration. Only a simple question,
about the origins of masturbation, that spun out of
control. The hand that embarks on accusation,
when the vagina is not looking, is the body's way
of claiming presence. The sea is too wide, too calm,
for argumentation to succeed. I dread the pink tokenism.

### *The Spectral Cow* (1928)

Again the dream of Breton reversed for the inane.
How may a cow dream of its impending transference
from symbol of rectitude to betrayer of tradition?
I see it stripped of its flesh, not yet groaning,
so far removed from the fallen bird, it claims land.

### *The Great Masturbator* (1929)

The style of sleep is bloat. The crotch hot and impotent,
ready to be sniffed. The grasshopper sings immortal
energy. The head inclines to the earth, snout-standing,
perversely ill. What fear then of women as they battle
phallic offensiveness? One sleeps through sex just as easily.

### *The Invisible Man* (1929-32)

All men are hoary constituents of leftover architecture.
Always the face bleeds into the ruins of buildings,
legs denote presumptuous waterfalls that no longer slide,
and the jug woman looks away, not interested in guarding
the pieces coming together moment to moment, fatedly.

### *Chocolate* (c. 1930)

"Beauty will always be edible." Jug, urn, in any case the spout
dribbles on the apple, affront to man in mode of devotion.

*Solitude* (1931)

We avoid looking into the face of the rock for all we're worth.
Welcome the shell, protected from useless talk, the calumny
of socialization. Would you throw your own wife over the cliff?

*The Persistence of Memory* (1931)

Gala protects you from the harsh outside (your crustacean shell)
so you can grow soft, supersoft, on the inside, invisible to all?
The truth is, watches are soft only in the way rocks are soft,
their interior harmony a question mark to spatial discord.
The clocks, if you note, must be wound before there is time.

*The Dream Approaches* (1932-33)

Take a blank canvas. Insert a coffin, women's genitalia, a naked
man on the beach with flames swirling on his back, a cracking tower,
dark cypresses, and the symbolism screams death of interpretation.
Once Freud put the apparatus in place dreams lost their thrill.

*The Architechtonic Angelus of Millet* (1933)

We permit prayer to turn our hearts into stone.
Where is the female of the species to warn of soliloquy?
The Catalonian landscape, heart-weary of dull potato farming,
observes the cosmic battle of the worn female,
pushing her conditional phallus out to the face.

*Necrophilic Spring Flowing from a Grand Piano* (1933)

Music calls us to our death. On one side, the cypress tree,
spouting from the hole in the piano, calling back to childhood,
on the other side, the pool of death. Music calls us to death.

*The Triangular Hour* (1933)

Your soft watch is becoming harder? Classical man watches
in feigned ignorance, unable to turn back to look at the plain.

*Hairdresser Depressed by the Persistent Good Weather* (1934)

Blocks of time, free of watches, yield unseen possibilities.
The primitive behind the hairdresser will yet wring joy
from Western cities, weather forecasting the new thrill.

*The Moment of Transition* (1934)

Our first bones will have been observed by the woman in white,
as we enter the new destiny of wherever villages turn to ruins.

*Allegory of an American Christmas* (1934)

America, Dalí, is new only in the sense that a cracked egg is.
I expect any moment for the north to turn gold too, in memoir.

*Paranoiac Face* (1935)

I would say the puzzle is in the unmaking of the human face.
We sit over our faces like huts in Africa puzzling animate cool.

*The Angelus of Gala* (1935)

You fear humble peasants praying over the potato harvest
as a "monstrous example of disguised sexual repression"?
You think the female would rather devour the poor male?
Fierceness in sexuality is a copout for you, Dalí, let it go.

*Autumnal Cannibalism* (1936)

War starts with soft slicing of the knife of one stone figure into
the other. Soon the pieces of meat devour us. Who is father,
who the son, only the rocks, which will outlast us, know for sure.

*Lobster Telephone* (1936)

It is better not to answer the phone if you think it might be Hitler.

### *The Burning Giraffe* (1936-37)

"The masculine cosmic apocalyptic monster" has been in the news
again. Woman loses features. We will die for the strip of meat.

### *The Invention of Monsters* (1937)

Premonition of war is the surrealist's first line of resistance.
A few months before the Anschluss, prophecy is a dead man's
only game. One head becomes two, everything twins.
While we sit counting butterflies, war doubles every silence.
The figures washing in the water look like horses from far,
the bust of the woman watched by the angel and the cat is horse
and woman. Something terrible waits for us, we foretell.

### *The Metamorphosis of Narcissus* (1937)

Those were the days when reflection repaid manifold.
There is no such pool of water left in the world, Dalí!

### *Sleep* (1937)

"Held up by the crutches of reality," you would have it,
sleep as the heavy monster, but where do the crutches
come from? We dream the crutches as props of reality,
we sleep into the dog-mind, we succumb to separation.

### *Impressions of Africa* (1938)

To concentrate on what is before us, we lose the outside.
Small conspiracies in dark lands are being hatched,
peasants strum handmade guitars. Don't put yourself
out, Dalí, bad news has a way of finding its means.

### *Invisible Afghan with the Apparition on the Beach of the Face of García Lorca in the Form of a Fruit Dish with Three Figs* (1938)

The death of Lorca interlocks apparitions for you, Dalí,
but the world counts him a romantic hero, whole, like an urn.

*Philosopher Illuminated by the Light of the Moon and the Setting Sun* **(1939)**

The same American Christmas egg, now in the shape
of an eclipsed dark moon? The philosopher studies his
fingernails, rocklike in emotion. The egg has cracked.

*The Enigma of Hitler* **(1939)**

Chamberlain did answer the phone, Hitler on the other end.
I would hang my umbrella too, paint swastikas on the backs
of all my wet nurses, if their backs were soft enough, like Hitler's.

*Daddy Longlegs of the Evening…Hope!* **(1940)**

Softness has become liquidity. I posit your dead tree figure,
the inkwells standing for female breasts, as mimetic scorn.
Must your phalluses always be held up by crutches?
Induced impotence, Dalí, is the first principle of war.

*Dream Caused by the Flight of a Bee around a Pomegranate,
a Second before Waking Up* **(1944)**

In dreams we float, we're told, because the air of reality
is too thin to anchor us. The moment before waking, with
the bayonet and the tigers aimed at the ethereal romanced
body, is also the moment of the end of carefree schooling.

*My Wife, Naked, Looking at Her Own Body, Which Is
Transformed into Steps, Three Vertebrae of a Column,
Sky, and Architecture* **(1945)**

No ordinary wife, Gala, evoked of stone and metal, classical
architecture personified, perfect shape of the back, all that you,
self-declared impotent, would consider the constituents
of a woman able to hold you in her cage, backbone to backbone.

### *Feather Equilibrium (Interatomic Balance of a Swan's Feather)* (1947)

"The atom was my favorite food for thought." Pity, after Hiroshima suspension would never be seen as mere freezing, giving you license to shatter the swan into head, foot, feather.

### *Dematerialization Near the Nose of Nero* (1947)

So you've become a classicist after all, Dalí? Is Nero coming together, head with bust, or splitting apart? How can your surrealism reconcile with atomic force, the greatest splitter? The thing to do is to stuff pomegranates in open cubes.

### *Raphaelesque Head Exploding* (1951)

Inside the Madonna's head, the Pantheon, the shapes clear despite the splitting, the ubiquitous rhinoceros horn, now in the service of illuminating religious devices.

### *The Sacrament of the Last Supper* (1955)

This ascension is mystical in the sense that an atomic bomb is.

### *The Dance (The Seven Arts, Rock 'n Roll)* (1957)

"I love anything that is dionysic, violent, and aphrodisiac." Dalí, you tire me. What happened to your impotence?

### *Tuna Fishing* (1966-67)

The battle has been deflected from man to fish. How I long for lobster telephones, Hitler on the other end! Do you now believe in finitude? Energy melts the personified universe.

### *Profile du Temps* (1984)

One last time, your soft watch, now almost bronzed with solidity, the bottom so close to melting we can taste it.

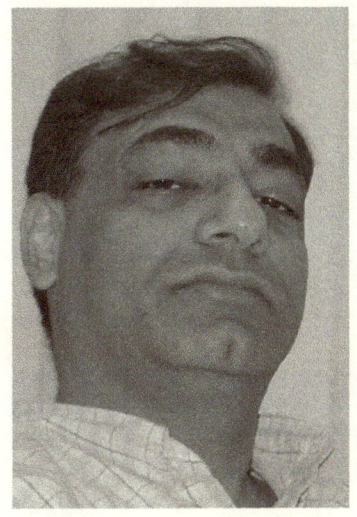

Anis Shivani is a poet, fiction writer, and critic in Houston, Texas. His books are *Anatolia and Other Stories* (2009), *Against the Workshop: Provocations, Polemics, Controversies* (2011), and *The Fifth Lash and Other Stories* (2012). He has also finished a novel, *Karachi Raj*, and is at work on another, *Abruzzi, 1936*. His work appears in *Georgia Review, Southwest Review, Boston Review, Iowa Review, Threepenny Review, Antioch Review, Michigan Quarterly Review, Agni, Denver Quarterly*, and many other journals.

The New York Quarterly Foundation, Inc.

New York, New York

## Poetry Magazine

**Since 1969**

Edgy, fresh, groundbreaking, eclectic—voices from all walks of life.

Definitely NOT your mama's poetry magazine!

The *New York Quarterly* has been defining the term contemporary American poetry since its first craft interview with W. H. Auden.

Interviews • Essays • and of course, lots of poems.

**www.nyquarterly.org**

No contest! That's correct, NYQ Books are NO CONTEST to other small presses because we do not support ourselves through contests. Our books are carefully selected by invitation only, so you know that NYQ Books are produced with the same editorial integrity as the magazine that has brought you the most eclectic contemporary American poetry since 1969.

## Books

**nyqbooks.org**

poetry at the edge™

www.ingramcontent.com/pod-product-compliance
Lightning Source LLC
Chambersburg PA
CBHW031137090426
42738CB00008B/1129